The
Female
Archangels

The Female Archangels

Reclaim Your Power with the
Lost Teachings of the Divine Feminine

CLAIRE STONE

HAY HOUSE

Carlsbad, California • New York City
London • Sydney • New Delhi

Published in the United Kingdom by:
Hay House UK Ltd, The Sixth Floor, Watson House,
54 Baker Street, London W1U 7BU
Tel: +44 (0)20 3927 7290; Fax: +44 (0)20 3927 7291
www.hayhouse.co.uk

Published in the United States of America by:
Hay House Inc., PO Box 5100, Carlsbad, CA 92018-5100
Tel: (1) 760 431 7695 or (800) 654 5126
Fax: (1) 760 431 6948 or (800) 650 5115; www.hayhouse.com

Published in Australia by:
Hay House Australia Pty Ltd, 18/36 Ralph St, Alexandria NSW 2015
Tel: (61) 2 9669 4299; Fax: (61) 2 9669 4144; www.hayhouse.com.au

Published in India by:
Hay House Publishers India, Muskaan Complex,
Plot No.3, B-2, Vasant Kunj, New Delhi 110 070
Tel: (91) 11 4176 1620; Fax: (91) 11 4176 1630; www.hayhouse.co.in

A catalogue record for this book is available from the British Library.

Tradepaper ISBN: 978-1-78817-362-9
E-book ISBN: 978-1-78817-367-4
Audiobook ISBN: 978-1-78817-385-8

Interior illustrations: www.jadehodesign.com

Printed and bound by CPI Group (UK) Ltd, Croydon CR0 4YY

To Mum, rest in the wings of the angels.
See you in my dreams.

Contents

List of Exercises

Chapter 9: Lady Mary

Chapter 10: Lady Shekinah

Chapter 11: Lady Seraphina

Who Are the Female Archangels?

*B*efore we get to know the female Archangels, the Archeiai (pronounced ar-kay-a), it's useful to understand their background. When we come to realize that we've only had access to half-truths of our history, the realms of possibility widen endlessly. The barriers that once held us down are now being lifted as wisdom and truths return to the people of Earth. Our eyes are truly awakening to the wonder of what we may be capable of achieving.

The fact that the feminine-natured angels were obscured in our past but are now growing in people's awareness holds great promise. There's everything to be gained from reaching our full potential when we remember who we really are: an eternal soul who sprang from the androgynous heart of creation.

As old paradigms shift at rapid speed, we're blessed to be guided and protected on this amazing journey into the unknown. Fumbling around in the dark can become a thing of the past – the light will always show us the way. The question is, will we allow ourselves to be carried on the wings of the angels?

The HuMAN Programming

Have you ever noticed that the major Archangels have masculine names? Almost everyone has heard of St Michael, Raphael and Gabriel, but how about Faith, Charity or Christine?

It's no coincidence that so little is known of these majestic beings. Worship of the Divine feminine can be traced back to the ancient origins of civilization. This was widespread for millennia before the Mother Goddess was wiped out of history intentionally. How else would patriarchy reign if humanity understood the power in unification of masculine and feminine energies? We've been spiritually fragmented by design. Those hungry for power began to divide us on a personal and global scale centuries ago, resulting in us being born into a man's world.

The majority of people go about their lives unquestioningly as to why they hold certain beliefs – and why would they? Unless they find themselves to be at rock bottom within a crisis or experiencing a spiritual awakening – which often go hand in hand – most people simply don't consider looking outside the box. This is because they're brain-trained to think that way.

When we were born, we were totally open and innocent. Even if we doubted what we were taught, constant repetition of suggestions made up our internal programming, reinforcing inherited be-LIE-fs into the subconscious mind. We generally live our lives based on the beliefs of our elders, which is why I call them be-LIE-fs; just because our grandparents believed something doesn't make it true.

We've reached a point in time where the scales of balance must weigh equally. The movements of the cosmos – the grand shift in ages – have heavily influenced our spiritual ascension, literally pushing us into an awakening. As the 2,160-year astrological cycle in Pisces comes to a close, the age of 'following the leader' is out and becoming our own guru is in. We're destined to be more than just sheep.

Guru means 'dispeller of darkness', and through analysing and healing our psychology we can repair and heal our souls, reclaiming our energy piece by piece until we achieve wholeness and enlightenment.

The angels are helping us with this huge quantum leap into the Golden Age of Aquarius - the prophesied age of the returned feminine. To make this shift, we must remember and reintegrate the lost ways of the feminine. Indigenous tribes, the Earth keepers, have always honoured Mother and Father God/dess equally. It's mainly us in the West who have been robbed of our Divine Mother, her mysteries and her wisdom.

After studying numerous man-made religions and coming up short every time, the female Archangels provided me with what I'd kept missing all along: the opportunity to retrieve my own wisdom. By learning to trust my intuition, and by following angelic guidance, I was able to reclaim my lost feminine power.

After seeking to know 'God' all of my life, the Archeiai brought me to realize that searching for God outside myself was like drinking from a half-filled cup - it was never going to be enough to quench my thirst. Only after reintegrating the feminine ways did I begin to touch the spark of God/dess that lay within me, at which point my cup became completely full, if not overflowing with alchemized life force - the Divine marriage of the soul.

The female Archangels hold the missing key to what we're seeking. They'll open the doors to all of the magic and mystery that was purposely hidden from us; because with it we're so incredibly powerful.

The Archeiai have helped me to achieve a state of balance by finally finding the middle path in life. Their lessons have served me very well: I've discovered how to heal my life, manifest my dreams and love myself. Most importantly, I've found inner peace. With nothing to search for any longer, I've learned to surrender to a constant process of slowly unfolding, for there's great joy to be found in the ability to accept all that is. Here, in this space, in the arms of the feminine, is where the real transformation takes place.

Now it's your time. You deserve to be happy, healthy and abundant. You can have all this and more. With the lost teachings of the feminine, the Archeiai will show you how to live purposefully, intentionally on track with your soul's destiny.

They're reaching out and the time is right - you're ready for this.

Why Now?

Although it appears that the female Archangels are new to working with us here on Earth, that's not true. They haven't made a grand appearance with the sole purpose of helping us birth our new golden age (although some have, like Lady Seraphina). The majority of the Archeiai have always assisted on our planet - they've stood by our side just as much as the masculine Archangels have - so why are we only hearing about them now?

There are two reasons that will answer this question. First off, like I said before, the female Archangels have been wiped out of history. Apart from a few references of female angels (in the Bible), they're not personally named and not much is said about them at all. This was intended to fit in with religion's take on how God is a man, the Archangels are male and women are made from a man, for man. Basically, disempowering women and all things feminine.

Secondly, we were unable to perceive them with our conditioned minds. This reminds me of the myth of the invisible ships of the Italian explorer Christopher Columbus. The story goes that when

Columbus' ships reached the land of the Americas, because they'd never seen them before and therefore had no concept of what one was, the native people were totally unable to see the ships. These kinds of stories are based on the theory that our perceptions are filtered – meaning that certain things go unnoticed by our conscious minds. This seems valid to me. It's well known that the eyes see many things that the mind fails to register. I expect we'd be quite overwhelmed with data to process if our brains brought everything to our attention. Furthermore, our brains fail to determine the difference between what is real and what is imaginary.

If we're raised in a masculine-dominant society, how could we perceive the feminine when we didn't even know that she was missing? We can only see what we believe is possible.

Now, it's time to awaken our inner eyes, to expand our capacity and to become the sovereign shining souls that we truly are.

The Venus Rose

The rose has long been associated with both the Divine feminine and the female Archangels. It's the highest vibrational flower that connects us to the pure heart of the universe: Venus.

The symbol on the cover of this book is the geometric pattern at the centre of the Venus Rose or the Pentagram of Venus. The planet of love makes this exquisite pattern after an eight-year journey of orbiting the sun 13 times. This pattern links us to the sacred pathway of the feminine as she dances in unison with the sun (masculine).

The Ascended Masters of Venus – the four Kumaras – work alongside the Archeiai as protectors of the feminine flame. Over the years, lightworkers and priestesses have served as conduits of this wisdom. The Hathors – Isis, Mother Mary and Mary Magdalene – are a few of the highest initiates of the flame; they each hold part of the wisdom of this great linage: the Sisterhood of the Rose. Guided by the Archeiai and the Goddess wisdom left behind by those before them, these women lived lives of devotion. In service to the Divine, they anchored the feminine flame upon Earth, touching lives where the angels couldn't. It's our birthright to reach this same level of mastery. The female Archangels are here to offer us as little or as much as we're ready to take.

Who Are the Female Archangels?

The female Archangels are known as the Archeiai – or simply have the word 'Lady' placed in front of their name. Throughout this book I call them Archeia/i, Lady and even Archangel interchangeably. It all means the same thing. Similarly, I refer to our Creator as God/dess, Source and universe; again, there's no difference in meaning. To me, they're just different terms used to represent the same thing – the loving omnipresent energy from which we all came and is inherent within all things.

To be as clear as possible, all angels are androgynous and beyond sexuality. You're now probably wondering how I've written an entire book on female Archangels when angels are above gender. Well, quite simply, it all comes down to energy. Masculine and feminine energy, to be precise.

You see, our entire universe is comprised of opposites: Yin and Yang, day and night, above and below, male and female, and so on. We're no different – in its highest truth, our souls are androgynous, too. Therefore, we have angels who are Divine feminine in nature and those who are Divine masculine in nature. Each equally important, these energies complement each other, hence the Archeiai being named the Divine Complements of the Male Archangels. Let me point out, the Archeiai aren't WAGS. They're not married to their 'other half' – they're what we'd call twin rays.

It's well known that each Archangel upholds the light of a specific ray. Let's use Archangel Michael as an example. 'He' contains and distributes the masculine energy of the blue ray, which includes protection, and gives us the confidence to speak our truth – these are the masculine qualities. Whereas Lady Faith upholds the feminine aspects of the blue ray, which include protecting ourselves and perhaps abstaining from speaking when something is better left unsaid.

Most of us have been trained to come from a place that's predominantly masculine. We rush, push and force. While these qualities serve us well at times, it's not natural to be in this state constantly. Knowing when to slow, surrender and wait are all qualities of the feminine. A balance of both allows us to embrace life fully while taking time to 'smell the roses'.

Balanced in energy, we get the chance to partake and observe. Like nature we, too, are able to accept the rhythms and cycles of life.

To apply the feminine qualities, we must go within and seek them out for ourselves. The Archeiai lead the way, but we have to do the work for ourselves. It's this style of teaching that will allow us to grow, so that we can become truly empowered and self-sufficient by following our own inner guidance and utilizing our special gifts.

If we all knew how to retrieve our own wisdom and knew when to rest or surrender, we'd live in a greater state of harmony. Being influenced by the distractions of the external world would become a thing of the past. Those in power knew this and intentionally disarmed us by taking away half of our power.

Men are included in this theft. They, too, have been suppressed of their feminine, leaving us with an epidemic of men who find themselves unable to express their emotions. Humans are half feminine and half masculine in energy. Enlightenment requires the Divine marriage of these energies, balanced in Yin and Yang.

There's no one to blame for our situation. We knew what we were signing up for. Our circumstances are always perfect for our soul's growth. The universe is always in harmony – whether we can perceive that or not. The cycles of life, death and rebirth continue eternally.

The Angelic Rays

The Archangels and their twin rays are individual identities yet, paradoxically, they're also one and the same. They're two polar opposite forces of nature that belong to the same ray of light. Imagine a scale of colour, where we have baby blue through to midnight blue, yet they're both still blue. We can also think of it as two sides of the same coin, or the two ends of a battery – two entirely different faces that are part of a bigger whole.

So far, there's a wealth of information on the masculine aspects of the angelic kingdom. This has served us so well and we'll continue to utilize the blessings of these mighty beings, but we're now at a pivotal point in our evolution. As we cross the threshold of the fourth dimension and beyond, we're ready for more!

There are lots of Archeiai who've come to light over the last 30 years or so. In this book, we'll be working with my personal favourites:

- Lady Ariel (pronounced air-re-el) – twin ray with Archangel Raziel (pronounced ra-zee-el)

- Lady Amethyst (pronounced ah-mu-thist) – twin ray with Archangel Zadkiel (pronounced zad-keel)

- Lady Aurora (pronounced ah-roar-ra) – twin ray with Archangel Uriel (pronounced you-re-el)

- Lady Charity (pronounced cha-ri-tee) – twin ray with Archangel Chamuel (pronounced sham-you-el)

- Lady Christine (pronounced chris-teen) – twin ray with Archangel Jophiel (pronounced jo-fee-el)

- Lady Faith (pronounced fay-th) – twin ray with Archangel Michael (pronounced my-kel)

- Lady Haniel (pronounced han-i-el) – twin ray with Archangel Nathaniel (pronounced nath-an-eel)

- Lady Hope (pronounced h-ope) – twin ray with Archangel Gabriel (pronounced gay-bre-el)

- Lady Mary (pronounced mare-ey) – twin ray with Archangel Raphael (pronounced raf-eye-el)

- Lady Shekinah (pronounced shek-ee-nah) – twin ray with Archangel Sandalphon (pronounced sandal-fon)

- Lady Seraphina (pronounced sera-fee-na) – twin ray with Archangel Seraphiel (pronounced sera-fee-el)

Each of these Archeiai is a keeper of specific spiritual heritage. They'll teach us how to put their ancient knowledge into practice, which will make us wise. The female Archangels will assist us in the creation of our best life. If we ask them, they'll be there to guide and protect us every step of the way as we unlock our unique gifts, including those of which we were unaware. If we take time out to do the inner work, our lives will transform beyond recognition and things will magically fall into place as we learn to dance with the rhythm of life.

There's an Archeia who can help us with every aspect of our life. Just like we may call upon Archangel Raphael to heal us, we can equally call upon his complement, Archangel Mary, to teach us how to heal. And rather than call upon Archangel Gabriel to grant our wishes, instead we can invoke Lady Hope to take us to the womb of creation to draw forth our own manifestations into being.

The Archeiai work with the exact same angelic rays as their masculine rays. However, they have very different ways in which they utilize these energies. Where's the fun if we keep getting others to make our magic for us? Believe me, making our own miracles is by far the greatest thing we can achieve on Earth. The best thing is, we can all do this – we were destined for greatness.

Archeia Names

We may read online other works giving an Archeia two names, such as Lady Hope aka Annunciata. While I neither support nor disagree with these names, the Archeiai who I work with have never introduced me to these double names, so I've kept it true to myself and used the one name that they've given to me.

We're all finding our way with the Divine feminine. With our heritage obscured, rules and guidelines can go out of the window – we must go within and follow what feels right for us individually. Like self-help author Dr Wayne Dyer says, 'Have a mind that is open to everything and closed to nothing,' which means we remain in a state of wonder and so a constant growth is available to us. Those who think they know everything limit themselves.

Every word and name holds a vibration. The names that we use to call upon the angels dictates the energy that we'll receive from them. Hope, Charity, Faith – how beautiful and pure are these names! Just saying them out loud awakens these virtues within us. So, say them often. Use them to conjure strength and wisdom that was always within us.

How to Use This Book

In this book you'll find a wide range of practical exercises. From dealing with negative thinking to entering the void of the universe, the basics must be covered in order to fly high.

I recommend that you read the book from start to finish, but when you're in need of guidance you can simply ask for a message and randomly open the book. Whichever angel or topic you open the page at will serve as advice as to which angel may best help you with your current issue. Use this book as an oracle.

Feel free to jump through the list of exercises in the front of the book – they can be used randomly rather than in a linear fashion. However, I highly recommend that you use the psychic protection exercises from the very beginning.

Be fully present with each experience. This means focusing all of your attention, thoughts and feelings on what you're doing at any given moment. If your attention wanders, just acknowledge this fact with kindness and bring your mind back to whatever you're doing at that precise moment. You can always focus on your breathing to bring your mind back to the present.

Some of the visualizations are very long. This is necessary to enable you to reach deep states of awareness. It may be a good idea to record them on your phone so you can play them back, following each step, or get a friend to read them out for you. That way they can also hold space for you.

If you don't yet see angels in their physical form, relax – you'll easily become accustomed to recognizing their energies by inviting them into your life and by working through the exercises within this book.

It's important to acknowledge that angels don't come 'dressed' in various outfits because they're fashion conscious; nor do they wear 'clothes' in the heavenly realms. The truth is that angels consist of pure energy, so in reality they're clothed in ethereal light. However, they'll cloak themselves in different 'bodies' and attire entirely for your benefit, as it serves as a form of non-verbal communication. Without even speaking to an angel, you can read them just as you'd read a card or a crystal ball. Their physical appearance, outfits, symbols, animals, flowers, colours or anything that they show you carry messages and hold symbolism towards what they wish you to know. If deciphering colours doesn't come easy to you, let go of attachments to colour – the angels will ensure that however you perceive the message will be perfect for you.

Sacred symbols that angels 'wear' serve as keys that unlock your superconscious mind to occult wisdom. Even the colours that angels are draped in affects and awakens your energy, bringing you healing and improved receptivity.

In this book, you'll experience working with several power animals as well as the angels. A power animal, also called a totem, is a spirit animal that will lend us their 'medicine' (unique qualities) to call upon in times of need. As well as our guardian angel and spirit guides, we have nine power-animal guides (one in the north, east, south, west, above, below and within, and two side by side). They've been assigned to assist us with our major life lessons. They help us to tap in to our talents and to achieve our soul path. For example, if one of our life lesson themes involves giving energy healing, you may well be paired with the spirit of the raven. These magical birds will eat up negative energy that may be present in your client's aura and give you potent visions of the past (to see how their psychic injury has manifested). Working with spirit animals is an ancient practice with its roots in shamanism. You'll find out more about these later.

Each angel has particular gemstones that are in energetic alignment with their specific areas of healing. Before you meet each angel, you can wear or hold any of the crystals listed within the chapter. This will help you to be more open to receiving information from the Archeiai directly, as they induce a deep state of relaxation and thus raise your vibrational frequency.

The universe is governed by a set of spiritual laws that we're encouraged to abide by. Choosing to follow them or not dictates whether we'll accrue positive or negative karma. You've probably heard of the Law of Free Will. The English dictionary describes the term 'free will' as 'the power of acting without the constraint of fate', meaning that how you act is your choice, as the forces of light (Creator) will leave you to experiment in the playground of life. This law also reminds us that we must ask an angel when we require their help, as they also subscribe to this law and so will never intervene without our permission.

Clearing Your Energy

Before you jump in to introduce yourself to the Archeiai, you may wish to familiarize yourself with the art of clearing your energy (aura and room space) by burning dried herb bundles. You'll probably be familiar with the term 'smudging' – a Native American tradition of burning dried sage (and other herbs) or even palo santo sticks in order to use their smoke in sacred ceremony. However, I recommend that you use herbs and plants that are native to your local region. The big trend of using imported sage and palo santo sticks has only been to the detriment to Mother Nature. Traditionally, the holy wood palo santo was only gathered from trees that had fallen naturally, the potent oils curing over years. Sadly, however, this practice is being heavily exploited so I urge you, please, to have respect for these sacred traditions and pick your own herbs - ones that are local to you.

It's very easy to dry and make your own herb bundles, and there's plenty of guidance online. And by doing so, your bundles will be infused with all the more magic! You'll also feel a deeper reverence and connection to Mother Earth as you've collected the herbs. Simply pick your herbs and plants (such as lavender, mugwort, rosemary) and hang them up to dry. They should be ready in about a week and then you can tie them up into bundles. You'll then use them in the exact same way as a smudge stick, whereby you light the bundle and pass the smoke through both your aura and your house, even over your oracle cards. This is a beautiful practice that will ensure you keep up good psychic hygiene. It'll clear your space and serve as an initiate (a beginning) into your prayers or meditations that follow.

Note: *Please consult a medical practitioner before working with herbs if you're pregnant, elderly, taking any medications or have a serious health concern.*

Working with Your Chakras

As you read this book you'll see that every Archeia corresponds with one or more of the chakras. While most people are familiar with the 7-chakra system, I also include two extra chakras – the Earth Star and the Stellar Gateway. These two energy centres are called transpersonal chakras as they're located outside the human body, unlike the traditional seven which reside directly through the centre of your physical body. The Earth Star is located around 30 centimetres (1 foot) below your feet and it grounds and connects you deeply to the earth plane. The Stellar Gateway is located around 30 centimetres (1 foot) above your head and it opens you up to the higher consciousness of the Divine. Together they enable you to create a successful bridge between the realms of heaven and Earth.

As human consciousness rapidly evolves, we gain the capacity to hold more light. In order to do so, we require more chakra centres to help us integrate the large quantity of high vibrational energy that's available to us. You'll hear people say that they're working on 7 chakras, 9 chakras, 12 chakras, or more. There's no right or wrong – we're each unique and at a different stage in our development. Just trust what feels right, and when it's time to upgrade your chakras, the angels will let you know!

Here's an overview to help you to remember where each chakra is located and which Archangel each is connected to.

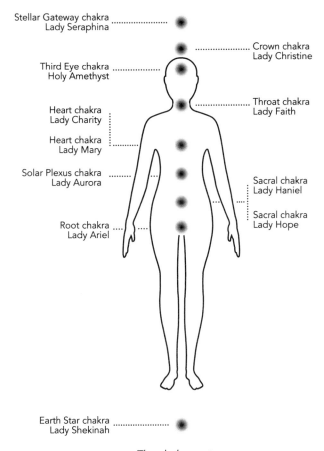

Stellar Gateway chakra
Lady Seraphina

Crown chakra
Lady Christine

Third Eye chakra
Holy Amethyst

Throat chakra
Lady Faith

Heart chakra
Lady Charity

Heart chakra
Lady Mary

Solar Plexus chakra
Lady Aurora

Sacral chakra
Lady Haniel

Sacral chakra
Lady Hope

Root chakra
Lady Ariel

Earth Star chakra
Lady Shekinah

The chakra system

A Final Word

Last but not least, enjoy yourself! Take your time with the process rather than rushing things. Reclaiming your sacred feminine self requires patience and trust. Know that you're exactly where you're supposed to be and that support is always available for you. All that's required of you is your permission – angels intervene by invitation only. So, what are you waiting for? Your Girl Guides await you.

CHAPTER 1

Lady Ariel
Lioness of the Goddess

Lady Ariel is one of the best known of the Archeiai and is much loved by many lightworkers. She has a strong connection to the Earth and was among the first of the female Archangels to make her presence known to humanity.

A natural leader, Lady Ariel helped to pave the way for the re-emergence of the Archeiai that would later follow, once the angelic gateway had widened alongside human consciousness. Her role on Earth has contributed hugely towards assisting and preparing our planet for the next step on humanity's ascension journey: the reclamation of the Divine feminine – the Goddess.

Clues to Lady Ariel's qualities can be found within her name, which translates as 'Lioness of the Goddess', 'Altar' and 'Hearth'. Each of these terms is a representation of her strength, magic and warmth.

Lady Ariel's Appearance

When Lady Ariel appears to me, she has the most mesmerizing green eyes and luscious long, fiery-red hair that gently floats around her white wings. Various colours of the rainbow bounce off her cool-pink aura, helping us to identify what it is within us that needs healing the most. For example, if we need inner peace, she'll emanate rays of green; if we need a boost of confidence, she'll embody an energizing red glow.

In times of fear or weakness, Lady Ariel has also appeared to me with the head of a lion. When she does this, it's to empower us and to remind us of our strengths and leadership abilities. She's saying, 'You've got this,' or 'Don't stand for this.'

Lady Ariel's Energy

Lady Ariel reminds me of the Strength Tarot card in that she doesn't allow fear to paralyse her. She understands the strength in overcoming obstacles by taming the lion through gentleness and femininity rather than using brute force to get our needs heard or met.

Lady Ariel is a peaceful warrior angel who can fill us with courage and willpower. Her vibrant energy whooshes in, enlivening and revitalizing us. She's the archetypal strict grandmother who takes no nonsense but loves us dearly. She'll push us to become authentic and true to ourselves.

Lady Ariel can help us with the following:

- finding courage

- healing the past

- offering practical support (career, finances)

- reigniting one's desire

- healing unfounded fears and anxiety

- providing links to ancestral karma

- accessing the prism of rainbow rays

- saying no

- manifesting your dream life

- guiding environmental projects

- offering prayers for sick animals

- healing your Root chakra

Lady Ariel's Calling Cards

Like all of the Archangels and Archeiai, Lady Ariel has signature calling cards that can be taken as signs or confirmation that she's around us. Here are a few of them:

- You may notice the number 888 or other formations of the number 8 appearing. You might see these on digital displays, such as on your phone, on clocks or even on bus numbers. You may notice that number of emails in your inbox or on a receipt. The number 8 also links to Lady Ariel because the eighth month (August) astrologically begins in Leo. The number 8 denotes infinity and abundance.

- Lady Ariel's animals are lions and all cats, big or small. After starting to work with her, you may see a child with a toy lion, or you may turn on the TV and see a wildlife documentary featuring lions.

- You may feel a physical rush of energy from your Root chakra.

- You may feel unusually confident or inspired to take action.

- Lady Ariel's flowers are dandelions and snapdragons, so your attention may be drawn to noticing these flowers somewhere.

Angel of Courage

Being the 'Lioness of the Goddess', Lady Ariel can help you to stand in your power and not become a pushover to manipulators or bullies. Sometimes we need to roar, but she'll guide us to express gentle assertiveness in a productive way rather than as an angry outburst.

Lady Ariel cuts to the chase and reveals truths that you might not want to look at and may even be hiding from yourself. This healing process empowers you to believe in yourself, pulls you out of stagnation and shifts you swiftly into clarity. Only from a clear point of view can you begin to dismantle rational or irrational fears that prevent you from achieving your heart's desires. Lady Ariel is also the perfect angel to call on if you find it hard to say 'no' or, as I once was, if you're suffering from anxiety.

Angel Encounter

I first met Lady Ariel when I was 14 years old. At the time, my mum was battling alcohol addiction and my life had become all about survival. I existed from day to day, putting all of my energy into looking after my three-year-old twin sisters. I was suffering from multiple panic attacks every day and was virtually a prisoner in my own home. I'd been living in this way for two years.

I knew I needed a miracle to help me with my mental health issues and in desperation, I asked the angels for help. Thankfully, my plea was heard and it was Lady Ariel who answered my call.

I remember it was night-time and that I'd spent a short time praying on my knees in my bedroom. Exhausted after another gruelling day of looking after my little sisters, I flopped on my bed. Tears rolled down my temples as I silently gazed up at the ceiling in expectation. Hoping. In my mind, I played a fantasy that I often used for comfort:

I imagined that God appeared and scooped me up into His arms. He reassured me that from now on, everything would be alright. He then carried me away to heaven, to safety, away from my terrible life.

Suddenly, in the middle of this fantasy, out of the corner of my eye I saw a rainbow of psychedelic colours. Shaking my head, I hoped I wasn't getting a migraine. But then the shimmering colours moved directly in front of me, forming the shape of a female angel. Although I jolted upright, I remained calm, as I'd encountered angels many times before.

The angel was so beautiful – she was dressed in a dazzling pink-and-gold robe and a multitude of colours gently twinkled all around her. The span of her white wings was at least 2 metres (6 feet), and all I could feel was an immense love as her green eyes gently gazed upon me.

Smiling, she spoke to me telepathically. In my mind, her gentle voice said:

> *Beloved child, I am the angel Ariel and I bring this message to you. We know you suffer now, but trust me when I say that your future is bright. There are many changes ahead and you will be happier than you could ever believe possible. You need to be strong a little longer. You can do this. Know that I am here every step of the way. All of this will help you one day when you are to be a leader.*

Lady Ariel then faded into the background, leaving me filled with a sense of renewed purpose. *What* will I be leading? I wondered. I couldn't even make it to the corner shop without breaking out in shakes and hyperventilating. I couldn't perceive this prophecy, but I was intrigued all the same.

From then on, each night when Lady Ariel came to visit me, I'd listen to her and act vigilantly upon every piece of guidance that she offered me. Within months, she'd taught me – a 14-year-old girl who didn't even attend school – how to heal my agoraphobia and anxiety without the help of conventional medicine, doctors, psychotherapists or even adults, for that matter. Lady Ariel is my heroine.

Lady Ariel is waiting to help *you* with all of your troubles: nothing is too small or large for the angels. Later on in this chapter, you'll get the opportunity to attune your energy with Lady Ariel's, so that you can communicate with her yourself. You can also partake in a fear-banishing ritual that I used when working with Lady Ariel to overcome my own fears.

Nature Angel

Lady Ariel is a very caring and warm-hearted angel. She adores wild flowers, aromatherapy oils and all the bounty gifted us by Mother Nature. She encourages us to enjoy them too, saying:

> *It is true that the best things in life are free. Take some time out to soak up blissful moments in nature – it is incredibly nourishing for the soul to sit by a crackling fire, walk barefoot on the grass, stargaze, nurse a baby, swim in a lake, climb a mountain or simply stroke a pet.*

> *Immerse yourself in as many magical moments as possible and be fully present within this experience – that is the true meaning of living heaven on Earth. Celebrate this practice by its simplicity – try it and I promise you that your soul will be washed with an incredible sense of peace, purpose and joy. Don't delay in taking some time out to sprinkle a little joy on your day.*

Lady Ariel reminds us that we share this planet. Nothing really belongs to any of us, for everything is either gifted or borrowed. And one day, like us, all things will return to the soil of Mother Earth once again.

The Earth's bounty is raped and abused by many, and Lady Ariel asks us to consider where in our lives we can show love and respect for our planet. You can do your part by making small gestures such as picking up litter from the street and recycling, or donating time or money to animal welfare groups or environmental projects and charities. By becoming as ecofriendly as possible, you help to protect all living creatures and future generations. It feels so good to be in nature and to appreciate her fully.

Lady Ariel acts as a protective mother of Gaia (Mother Earth) and all of the children who rest upon her. This includes us as human beings and all other mammals, insects, sea creatures, plants and trees, as well as the elementals (fae, salamanders, sylphs, gnomes, water spirits, undines and elves).

Working so closely with the elemental beings means that Lady Ariel is one of the few angels who govern all elemental energies equally:

- Her powers of fire can cool down a fiery temper or stoke flames of inspiration.
- Her powers of earth can ground your energy into the here and now and plant seeds of intention into the fertile soil of manifestation.
- Her powers of water cleanses and nourishes your spirit, connects you to the feminine and heightens your intuition.
- Her powers of air helps you to become clear in your thinking and aligns you with the great mind of Source.

Having an energetic affinity with all of the elements (like the magician in the Tarot deck) makes Lady Ariel one of the most magical angels. If there's a way to manifest your dream reality, she's the angel who'll orchestrate synchronistic events to ensure optimal chances of success.

Angel of Magic

Lady Ariel is available to more than just the greats, though. She's also here for you and can help you in very practical ways. She can ensure that you're in the right place at the right time; she can conjure resources such as money or childcare; and she can empower your thinking so that you adopt a positive attitude and self-belief. Lady Ariel helps us to align with the truth of who we are and what we came here to do. She says, 'There are no excuses except those imposed upon us by ourselves!'

The Magical Duo

It wasn't until 2011 that I realized that Archangel Raziel and Lady Ariel had merged into the same angelic ray. Previously, I'd believed them to be entirely separate – I was unaware of their very deep connection.

I was becoming increasingly curious about the Archeiai and one day I simply posed a question to Lady Ariel: Do all angels have a counterpart? Lady Ariel's pink-and-gold energy began to glisten and deepen in colour, and I detected the sweet scent of geranium as I inhaled deeply. Slowly, her face began to change form. Before I could ask her what she was doing, she'd transformed into Archangel Raziel. He smiled at me as I sat wide-eyed and speechless.

In that instant it made perfect sense to me: Archangel Raziel explained that all of the Archeiai are beginning to shape strong identities on Earth, totally independent of their male Archangel counterpart. He excitedly told me that eventually, all of the Archeiai will be felt as strongly as Lady Ariel is now, as a sovereign, feminine, shining one.

I was absolutely fascinated to hear this radical information first-hand. I realized that even after all of my years of communicating with the angels, and considering myself an angel expert, what I knew was just the tip of the iceberg.

Archangel Raziel

Archangel Raziel's name means 'Secrets of God'. Like the lion who guards the royal crown on coats of arms, he's the guardian of all of the wisdom, knowledge, secrets and mysteries of both the universe and creation. He's the Divine alchemist, quantum physicist and magician.

If you've seen the *Harry Potter* movies, you can think of the magical duo of Archangel Raziel and Lady Ariel as the angelic elders of Hogwarts to get an idea of their personality. Archangel Raziel has also spent physical lifetimes on Earth and in one of his incarnations he lived the life of the Ascended Master Merlin. He spent that lifetime as an advisor to King Arthur and, most importantly, alongside the Knights Templar, he protected the sacred lineage of the Sisterhood of the Rose.

Archangel Raziel comes forth now, playing his part in revealing the truth of who we truly are to all those who are ready to remember and embrace our lost spiritual heritage. He can help you to tap in to your own psychic abilities by overlighting your aura as you practise your 'clairs': clairaudience, claircognizance, clairempathy, clairgustance, clairsalience, clairsentience, clairtangency and clairvoyance.

When Archangel Raziel appears to me I see him as a very tall and slender angel. His features are somewhat feline-looking, his green eyes glistening in contrast to his dark skin. He wears a gold-and-indigo robe and a myriad of rainbow colours cascade through him from top to bottom. Sometimes, like Archangel Raphael, he's depicted with a caduceus or a sceptre, which represents his unique ability to shapeshift through any of the angelic rays.

The Superconscious (God/dess)

The name Raziel is an anagram of Ariel, but with the extra letter Z. During a channelled writing session, Archangel Raziel revealed the following information to me to help me to better understand how to enter the mind of God/dess:

> The letter Z in my name represents the direction in which energy travels through the mind (brain) when you become one with the mind of God/dess. Our consciousness travels from unconscious to conscious and back again.
>
> If we can keep these parts of the mind open simultaneously, we then access a third state of consciousness, known as the superconscious mind. This state of mind can be attained through spiritual practices such as yoga, chanting or breathwork.

Referring to Harry Potter once again, I find it interesting symbolically that Harry gains his Z-shaped scar on his forehead (Third Eye chakra) when he's 'struck' into an awakening of his supernatural gifts. What gifts would you like to reawaken within you? Before you go to sleep at night, ask Archangel Raziel to take you to his mystery school, where you can learn about them during your dreamtime.

Working with Lady Ariel

Now that you know the basics about Lady Ariel and what she specializes in, I bet you're really looking forward to meeting her, if you haven't already. To enhance your connection to Lady Ariel, you may like to use a few simple items or create a basic altar to correspond with her energy. I recommend working with a red- or orange-coloured altar cloth, clothing or candles, and burning black pepper or Roman chamomile essential oils. In addition to these optional extras, next is a list of Lady Ariel's gemstones:

Lady Ariel's Gemstones

The following crystals have the healing vibrations that resonate with the work of Lady Ariel:

- rubellite

- ruby

- rainbow moonstone

- Herkimer diamond

- tiger's-eye

Try this next mini ritual to introduce yourself to the wonderful healing presence of Lady Ariel. Connecting to her energy will help you to be courageous and stand in your power. She'll also add extra valour to your intentions:

 ### INVOCATION: CALLING IN LADY ARIEL

As with other longer exercises in the book, you may like to record yourself reading the text of this ritual on your phone and then play it back, following each step.

You will need:

- ~ a white candle

- ~ matches

- ~ a pen and a piece of paper

- ~ a dried herb bundle

When you're ready to call in Lady Ariel, find a quiet place where you can sit in peace and relax. Take a few deep breaths to calm and centre yourself, then begin:

~ First, light your herb bundle and pass the smoke through your aura with the intention of clearing any tension and negativity.

~ Whisper 'Lady Ariel' three times.

~ Say, 'Lady Ariel, Lady Ariel, Lady Ariel.'

~ Light a candle in her honour.

~ Raise your vibration by thinking of happy thoughts or memories.

~ Take eight deep breaths, in through your nose and out through your mouth.

~ Say, 'Archeia Ariel, Divine Lioness of Light, please lend me your courage and strength so that I may step into my own sacred feminine powers, enabling me to shine the light of my truth brightly. Use me to illuminate the pathway for others to discover their own truths and divinity.'

~ Now, imagine a huge, radiant diamond made of light appearing before you.

~ It begins to rotate slowly and with each turn, all of the colours of the rainbow burst out, one by one, washing over you from head to toe and penetrating every cell in your body.

~ Once your body is totally filled up with the diamond's light, expand it outwards into your aura.

~ Breathe deeply as an energetic casing forms over you, offering you protection.

~ Now, draw your awareness to the Root chakra at the base of the spine.

~ Direct healing diamond energy to this energy centre with the power of your breath.

~ Imagine the Root chakra as a glowing red rosebud.

~ As the petals peel back, a crystal doorway emerges in the centre of the rose.

~ The door is encrusted with glistening rubies and rose quartz crystals.

~ You realize that this is the entrance through this chakra's portal.

~ Allow your consciousness to travel through the doorway by simply imagining yourself walking through the door.

~ You enter a tropical land of luscious greenery and pink crystalline temples.

~ You spot a glistening rose quartz throne in the centre of a quiet courtyard.

~ The head of a dazzling golden lion is embellished on the throne.

~ Placing your hands over your heart, call Lady Ariel's name once more.

~ She appears from behind a bush of red roses and embraces you with her white wings.

~ She motions you to sit upon the throne.

~ Share your dreams, hopes or issues with Lady Ariel now.

~ After placing a crown of red roses on your head, Lady Ariel gives you a direct message – trust whatever comes into your mind right now.

~ Spend as much time as you like exploring her magical garden.

~ Retrace your steps back to the crystal door, which closes firmly behind you after you've passed back through.

~ The petals of your Root chakra close over.

~ Take a deep breath in and when you're ready, thank Lady Ariel.

~ Write down all that you've seen and go back to visit often.

Congratulations! You've just journeyed through the Root chakra gate with Lady Ariel. You can travel back to this place any time you're anxious or could do with a top-up of energy in this area.

Now that you've connected with Lady Ariel, you're ready to use the following exercises to help you to overcome your fears and to let go of anything standing in the way of manifesting your desires. Lady Ariel reminds you to give something back every time the universe answers your prayers. You can have very little money and still be liberal with love or generosity. Here's a simple water blessing that you can incorporate into your daily routine:

Water Blessing

A great way of giving something back is to get into the habit of blessing water. It's so quick and easy that everyone can do it, even children. We don't need Lady Ariel to remind us of our ever depleted and polluted oceans – we already know that the waters are in desperate need of our prayers. We also know that water imprints energy patterns of memories within it.

By simply holding your hand over a glass of water before you drink it and saying 'May this water be blessed and filled with love,' you're drinking the molecule of love! Your blessings then imprint the vibration of love into your cells.

If you do the same over your bathwater, every layer of your energetic bodies will bask within the matrix of love. Once the water goes down the drain, it'll spread its love program to other water molecules that it comes into contact with.

Spread love and blessings wherever you go by blessing all water. Say either, 'Lady Ariel, may the angels of nature flock to Earth now, restoring our oceans with clean water for our sea creatures to flourish. And so it is.'

Or, 'May this water be blessed with love, spreading love wherever it touches. Amen.'

Offering your prayers for the good of others with no expectation of anything in return, even thanks, is an act of true devotion and service. This is because if you expect something in return and are only doing it for this reason, you're actually doing it for yourself, rather than the good of the other person. Remember how good it feels to give to another cause. It's incredibly rewarding when you make a difference in the world and it's good for your health! In her book *The Power of Eight*, Lynne McTaggart, an expert on the science of spirituality, details experiments in which those who prayed for others had less chance of developing disease and therefore lived longer than those who either didn't pray at all, or those who only prayed for themselves.

Lady Ariel says that you have the right to be devoted to yourself and your true life purpose. But this is often easier said than done. The disenfranchisement of women has led to many of us holding back from our heart's desires. Perhaps we'd feel guilty pursuing our passions, or maybe we've subscribed to another person's be-LIE-fs of what it means to be a woman. This way of thinking is outdated. It's time to rise. Let's look at what's holding you back from your chance of being the best version of you.

Ariel the Courageous

Lady Ariel encourages us to look at our fears and decide if they're serving us or not. She stands for empowerment and the maxim by Susan Jeffers: 'feel the fear and do it anyway'. Contemplate this: how many times have you put off doing things to avoid facing your fears? Isn't it true that most of the time we over-anticipate events that are out of our comfort zone, our mind amplifying all that could go wrong rather than focusing on what could go right? How many times have you confronted a fear to later wonder what all the fuss and worry was about? Most of the time, the things we thought would terrify us end up not being so bad, after all.

Getting to the root of your fears is key to overcoming them. Often, the uncovering alone is enough to transmute them; other times you may need additional support. I like to perform mini rituals when I require an extra boost.

The following candle magic ritual is very simple and produces magnificent results. You'll need to choose keywords that sum up your fears and when you're ready, release them once and for all. Candle magic is a very simple yet extremely powerful way of working with angels and the powerful elements of Fire and Air. Air will help you to focus and have a direct mindset, while Fire will cleanse away any fears that it meets.

TRANSMUTE YOUR FEARS WITH CANDLE MAGIC

For this exercise, you'll only need a few 'magical tools':

~ an intention: what do you wish to release?

~ a black candle (black is the colour for banishing)

~ matches

~ a toothpick

~ a sharp knife or athame (for carving)

~ cedarwood essential oil (a powerful consecrator)

~ a dried herb bundle or incense stick

Before you start, light your dried herb bundle or an incense stick and waft the smoke over your magical tools to consecrate them, then follow the next process:

~ Centre your energies by taking a few deep breaths in through the nose and out through the mouth.

~ Let your muscles become heavy and imagine that the air you're breathing travels in through the front of your Root chakra.

~ As you exhale, imagine your breath exiting through the back of the Root chakra.

~ If visualization isn't your strong point your concentration and intention is still a great place to start.

~ Call in Lady Ariel to invoke her protection and courage.

~ Say, 'Lady Ariel, Lady Ariel, Lady Ariel. Thank you for being here with me now and for standing by my side, filling me with your protection, love and courage.'

~ Imagine her white wings wrapped around you, gently hugging you.

~ Take the carving tool of your choice and the candle.

~ Spelling the words backwards, carve the name of the fear you wish to overcome into the candle (for example, SHAME would be EMAHS).

~ Hold the base of the candle in your right hand and the wick in your left.

~ In your mind or out loud, state the following: 'Lady Ariel, thank you for embodying me with your strength and love. May I now overcome this fear of [state your fear], knowing that all is well and I'm safe at all times, and so it is.'

~ Rub the cedarwood oil over the carvings and light the candle.

~ Leave it until it burns out (remember to be candle safe: keep an eye on them and remain in the room at all times when lit).

Together with Lady Ariel, the cleansing flames, magical ingredients and your powerful intention, you'll begin to clear your blockages and fears. You can inscribe more than one fear onto your candle; however, it's more powerful to add one at a time and repeat the process.

Many of my clients have worked through their blockages to summon the courage to walk their chosen life path only to find that they aren't financially supported. Does this sound all too familiar to you?

My client 'Ruth' was in her 30s and had experienced a difficult childhood. Her parents had largely ignored her and when they did interact with her, it was to put her down – they often told her she was stupid. Owing to her rejection as a child, Ruth had a very deep-seated feeling of unworthiness and as a result found it very difficult to manifest abundance as an adult.

With the guidance of Lady Ariel, I helped Ruth to examine the root cause of her limiting beliefs, which of course were formed by opinions of herself and others (teachers, parents) as a little girl. In her adult life, the internal program of her be-LIES weren't actually true and now, with the realization of where these ideas came from, Ruth was able to free herself. She was then able to reset the hardwired program that her subconscious mind was constantly replaying and keeping her from being open to receiving. We used meditations, affirmations and inner child work to heal Ruth's cycle of attracting experiences of lack.

The result? With no extra effort, Ruth was offered a promotion at work, she received an unexpected tax rebate that allowed her to clear her credit card and she even won a huge Easter hamper at her child's school fair. Now that's pretty amazing for someone who'd only been clearing her abundance blockages for just a few weeks!

You could use the magic ritual using a candle (earlier) to transform any negative beliefs that you hold surrounding wealth and worthiness. Another empowering technique to instil you with the courage or drive to achieve your desires is to embody the shamanic 'medicine' (qualities) of Lady Ariel's animal, the lion. Shamans call upon the 'medicine' of an animal to help members of their tribe. They may connect with this animal to assist with a hunt, to protect the tribe or to receive visions from other realms.

As well as your guardian angel and spirit guides, you also have personal power animals. You can call upon the power of any animal to 'borrow' its qualities and strength. With permission, you can draw these powerful energies into yourself. For example, if you felt under attack from bullies, you could call upon an armadillo to shield you. If you wanted to go unnoticed, you'd call upon a chameleon to blend in.

Lady Ariel is connected to all physical and spirit animals. Try this shamanic exercise to become the Lioness of the Goddess yourself:

THE SHAMANIC ENERGIES OF THE LION

As I stated earlier, you can 'call in' the strengths and traits of specific animals to help you to swiftly move through life's challenges. To be in keeping with the energy of Lady Ariel, this exercise is intended to allow you to experience strength, courage and bravery. Here, you will embody the swift lion.

You will need:

~ a white candle

~ matches

~ a pen and a piece of paper to hand for taking notes afterwards

When you have your items, light your candle and begin:

~ Centre your energies by taking several deep breaths in through the nose and out through the mouth.

~ Ground your energies by sending roots from the soles of your feet deep into the Earth.

~ Call in Lady Ariel by saying, 'Lady Ariel, Lady Ariel, Lady Ariel.'

~ As she appears before you, see her wearing a golden helmet that resembles a lion's head.

~ Visualize two lions stood either side of her.

~ Next, state your intention: 'Lady Ariel, thank you for attuning my energies to the spirit of the majestic lion. May I know how it feels to be your strength and grace.'

~ Visualize Ariel removing her helmet and placing it over your head.

~ You immediately feel the raw, poised life force racing through your veins.

~ One of the lions steps forwards.

~ Ask her to blend with your aura by stepping into your energetic field.

~ *Become* the lion – how does it feel?

~ Move around and even crawl on the floor or roar – totally let loose.

~ Does the lion have a message or a gift for you?

~ Trust that whatever comes to mind is perfect for you right now.

~ When you've finished, totally disconnect your energy from the lion by imagining her pulling away and returning to Lady Ariel.

~ Bring your roots back in and stamp your feet on the ground a few times.

~ Have a drink and a bite to eat to bring you back to the here and now.

Whenever you need to face an uncomfortable challenge, imagine the lion helmet pulled over your head. Channel the lioness power.

Angel of Abundance and Prosperity

With all of the energy I squandered on my anxiety disorder all those years ago, I found it very hard to manifest abundance. This situation is common and it can trigger strong feelings of fear. The Root chakra is knocked out of sync when we remain in a place of fear.

You might be in the same position that I was in back then – no matter how hard I worked, it seemed that I could only just keep my head above water financially. I'd read so many books about the Law of Attraction - recited the affirmations, practised feng shui in my home – and still nothing changed. I never quite had enough.

Then I asked Lady Ariel to explain *why* I was struggling to accept prosperity. In a vision, she showed me that in many of my past lives I'd taken vows as nuns and monks and had promised to give all of my possessions away. It was respectable to be poor.

If you're struggling with prosperity and it's triggering fear, the following exercise can help you. Perhaps you, too, have made vows of poverty in previous incarnations (past lives). This is the exact exercise that Lady Ariel went through with me to help me to discover how my own past lives were impacting on my current life:

RITUAL TO RELEASE POVERTY VOWS

For the next exercise, gather the few items required and find a space where you'll be comfortable and undisturbed.

You will need:

~ approximately 15 centimetres (6 inches) of red ribbon

~ a pen and two sheets of white paper

~ dried herb bundle for burning

When you're ready, proceed:

~ Take a few slow deep breaths in through your nose and out through your mouth to centre your energies and then call upon Lady Ariel.

~ Say, 'Lady Ariel, Lady Ariel, Lady Ariel, I call upon your Divine presence.'

~ Close your eyes and feel or see Lady Ariel's loving presence enter the room.

~ Spend some time absorbing her beautiful energy until you feel happy and relaxed.

~ You're now going to ask Lady Ariel to reveal to you whether or not you've taken vows of poverty (most of us have).

~ In your mind's eye, imagine her handing you an ancient scroll.

~ The scroll states your vows.

~ Read them, trusting whatever comes to mind.

~ If you're visual, you may even see memories of events (or snatches of them), along with your signature.

~ Write down your findings on a sheet of paper.

~ Waft the smoke of your herb bundle over what you've written, to cleanse and release.

~ Say three times: 'With Lady Ariel as my witness, I am now free from all vows, made across all planes and times of existence, and so it is.'

~ Closing your eyes once more, imagine her setting the scroll alight until your name and the promises have totally vanished.

~ Complete the freedom-granting process by destroying the physical sheet of paper – you could burn it in the fire, or shred and discard it.

~ Next, physically write a new contract for yourself in this lifetime.

~ On the second piece of white paper, write: 'I [your name] now agree to a life filled with love, prosperity and abundance. Like everyone else, I deserve and choose to have my needs met.'

~ Now, sign the contract!

~ Roll the paper up like a scroll and tie it with the ribbon.

~ Keep it in a safe place, away from others, so that it contains the energy of your wish.

~ Look at it each morning to remind you of the life you wish to lead.

~ Express your gratitude to Lady Ariel with a simple 'thank you'.

Remember, in order to manifest consciously, you first need to wipe the energetic slate clean. Then you can plant your seeds of intention in fresh soil, where they'll be nurtured, free from the weeds of your mind.

Along with the contract, it's important that you keep your thoughts focused and positive. Affirmations are a great way to reprogram your mind:

PROSPERITY AFFIRMATIONS

Say the following mind-programming affirmations daily to become a magnet for abundance. Ensure that all of your statements are said in the positive and present tense, like below:

~ 'I am abundant'

~ 'I am rich'

~ 'I am a magnet to money'

~ 'The more I give, the more I receive'

~ 'Money follows me'

~ 'I am surrounded by abundance'

~ 'There is always enough'

~   'My needs are always met'

~   'I deserve to live a comfortable life'

The beauty of reciting affirmations is that nothing special is required to utilize them and you can do them anywhere! Think about what you want to affirm (confirm that it's true) and make up your own positive affirmations. To add that extra zest, try saying them while looking in the mirror. Looking into your own eyes is a powerful practice – your soul will know you mean business.

Working with Lady Ariel can help you to gain the confidence to go for it in life. She keeps your feet on the ground and out of the ego by reminding us to be generous and loving to all creatures. The small voice of the ego will give you all of the excuses you need to play it small, while the voice of the soul will encourage you to dream big and step out of your comfort zone. You deserve to have an amazing life! Lady Ariel will help you to believe it and achieve it.

CHAPTER 2

Holy Amethyst
Wholeness of the Goddess

Lady Amethyst, also known as Holy Amethyst, is the Archeia of the Violet Diamond Light of Alchemy and Transmutation.

Her name 'Holy' derives from the word 'whole' and reflects how she can help you to become energetically complete by transcending the five senses and by freeing you from any energy feeders. Amethyst in Greek means 'non-intoxicated' or 'not drunk'. This part of her name represents the deep clarity of self that she can help you to obtain once your energy is 'sober' – clear, high vibrational and untouchable.

Holy Amethyst's Appearance

Being one of the keepers of the sacred Violet Flame makes her one of the go-to angels for transmutation of any kind. Once your energy is crystal clear, she'll assist you in slowly piercing the veils of illusion, inducing a psychic awakening.

Lady Amethyst appears to me with a pale white skin tone and piercing, violet-coloured eyes. She's swamped from head to toe in dozens of glorious shades of lavender, lilac and all kinds of purple. This includes her long silky robe, her flowing hair and even her wings! She wears a large oval-shaped amethyst necklace that hangs low over her Heart chakra.

What I find so fascinating about Holy Amethyst is how her crystalline heart 'beats' out. Silver strands of energy literally pulse out of her like streaks of electricity. After rippling into her sphere, the energy settles upon her huge aura, creating the most beautiful tapestry of light you've ever seen.

Holy Amethyst's Energy

Like all of the angels, Lady Amethyst has a lovely peaceful feel to her energy. When she comes in you'll feel very serene yet mentally on form at the same time. Most people experience their intuition increasing, making her the angel you'll most likely physically 'see'. It's common to have goose bumps breaking out on your skin and you may also hear high-pitched tones as her energy stimulates your sixth senses of clairvoyance (clear vision) and clairaudience (clear hearing).

In the Tarot deck she's similar to The High Priestess archetype. Her psychic powers make her the all-seeing and all-knowing wisdom keeper. However, she's also the keeper of secrets, so she'll only impart esoteric knowledge to those who'll use it with integrity and for the highest good of all beings.

Lady Amethyst can help you to anchor fundamental spiritual basics into the foundations of your persona, such as conscious listening and speaking. She's the angel of silence and can teach you how to hear with your 'higher' or 'inner' ears, which receive untainted information, unlike the 'ego' or 'outer' ears, which have a tendency to judge.

Another basic skill that she'll help you to develop is the ability to maintain your quiet, which is especially good if you're trying to give up the gossip or if you struggle to hold your tongue! She'll provide you with a purple spark of light right before your eyes, to serve as a reminder as to when to keep information to yourself. When you're about to share knowledge with an untrustworthy person, she'll give you a very clear warning sign. Twice, Lady Amethyst has used the song 'Don't Speak' by the band No Doubt by bringing it to my attention on the radio. Both times I heard it just in the nick of time, before I divulged information to people who didn't have my best interests at heart. At other times she's brought my attention to Stop road signs, the TV advert for the Silentnight bed brand and so forth, you catch my drift…

It's very important to understand that Lady Amethyst wants you to promote your truth rather than repress it by keeping schtum, which is far more productive. Her guidance is aimed at helping you to be more accurately received and understood.

She realizes that at times it can be very easy to get swept up by your emotions. With this in mind, she very simply points out that there could be a better time and place to express yourself.

She can help you with:

- clearing your energy of lower frequencies
- clearing past-life residue
- clearing ancestral karma
- developing your psychic gifts
- enhancing your intuition
- being honest
- transcending temptation of the sensory pleasures
- accessing wisdom from higher dimensions

- alchemizing your mind, body and spirit

- balancing the Third Eye chakra

- seeing tasks through to the end

- healing addictions

- increasing your listening skills

Holy Amethyst's Calling Cards

You may notice some of the following signs when you're working with Lady Amethyst:

- The number formation of 99, 999 and 9999 is in alignment with the energetic frequency of Holy Amethyst, where 9 is the magic number! It shows up when final snags and tweaks need to be completed, yet you feel as though you're running out of steam to conclude them. Lady Amethyst can inspire you to see the job through to the end by giving you glimpses of how the future could look.

- Her animal totems are snakes and scarab beetles, both symbolizing spiritual rising, alchemy and the shedding of old skins. Snakes can hear with their whole body. They're so good at listening that they can predict a natural disaster weeks before it happens.

- When you're in her presence you may well feel a hot, tingling sensation on your forehead.

- When working with her you usually develop a no-nonsense attitude. With such deep clarity you're able to make decisions easily and act upon your urges with trust and unwavering faith in yourself.

- Her flowers are lavender and African violets – both flowers of purification.

Angel of Transmutation

Lady Amethyst says that just like reducing our carbon footprint, we should also try to refrain from leaving a toxic energetic trail behind us on Earth. She says, 'Let us leave nothing but traces of love wherever we have been.' She conveys this message to us in a very light-hearted manner because she knows that in our human form, we're here to experience a variety of emotions, which of course makes it impossible for us never to have a negative thought or a cross word with someone.

However, we still have to clean up after ourselves! By adopting the positive habit of clearing and transforming our energy and mindsets we free the future generations from taking on our wounds. We also shield them from limitations that we might have inherited from our ancestors. The lineage of suffering can end with us – we have the power to protect our children and the future generations from inheriting our karma, diseases and traits.

Holy Amethyst can help you to transmute anything that lowers your vibration, from a simple negative thought to evil entities that may attempt to penetrate and feed from your aura. Her lilac aura in the guise of a flame will swiftly swallow up darkness and replace it with light – she's a true alchemist.

Very often, she teams up with Archangel Michael to assist those in need of psychic protection and energy clearance. Holy Amethyst transmutes psychic debris and Archangel Michael seals off the aura, shielding it from further invasion. I've worked with this duo of angels many times when I've given healing treatments and especially when I used to clear houses of unwanted energies. They're the standard angel toolkit for all therapists and psychics.

Angel Encounter

I have a very close bond with Holy Amethyst. As far back as I can remember, I've always known her. The story that I'm about to share with you is a more recent encounter and serves as a great example of how you can work with her.

I received my reiki attunements back in 2001 and immediately set up my own mobile healing practice. The angels soon began adding their magical energy to the mix. I'd open up a space in which they could enter and my winged friends would then use me as a vessel to channel their healing energy to my clients. They'd also provide me with insight into what needed healing and why, which was always golden information.

That's why I decided to call my offering 'Angelic Healing' rather than reiki. The angels deserve some credit for all of the contributions they've made and continue to make to my work.

I absolutely love giving healings, but the moment I answered the phone to 'Kelly' I immediately felt anxious. Still, I offered her an appointment for the angelic healing that she'd enquired about, despite the fact that my gut instinct was screaming a big, loud 'no'. I wasn't sure why I didn't want to work with her, but not having much of a voice back then I agreed regardless.

As the appointment day drew closer, I grew increasingly concerned about meeting her. Even so, always keeping my promises, I felt obliged to proceed with the meeting.

As soon as her car pulled up on my driveway, I sensed that something was off. A wave of panic overcame me as the realization hit me that an unsavoury energy was about to enter my beautiful home – the place that was a safe haven to my children… to me! My spirit guide Helena told me to snap out of it. It was then that the answer came to me and I knew exactly what to do. I'd already called in protection from Archangel Michael, which was standard practice for me, but I knew if I was going to help this woman, I was going to need even more backup.

I called in the perfect girl for the job: Holy Amethyst. Instilling me with confidence, I knew that with my team I'd got this. Holy Amethyst began by placing a Violet Flame shower over me. She has a very dry sense of humour, so I took it as a joke at first, until it dawned on me that my own fears had contaminated my aura and I did indeed now need purifying myself. No sooner had the purple light rays finished raining down over me than she called in the violet fire dragons, which swept through and around the house, blazing away, transmuting as they went.

Finally, Holy Amethyst began to create a blazing wall of violet fire over my front doorway as security. We set it up with the intention of instantly zapping away any negative energy that it met, thereby preventing anything unwanted from crossing my threshold.

The doorbell rang and I welcomed Kelly – only Kelly – into the house. She'd driven a very long way to get to me and asked if she could use my bathroom. While she was in there, Lady Amethyst told me to do something strange. She instructed me to take a photograph of Kelly's car outside. Feeling like a secret agent, I slipped outside to the front of the house and took a quick snap. To be honest, I did feel a little uncomfortable doing so, but I trusted Lady Amethyst's guidance unquestionably.

As I performed the treatment on Kelly, she openly admitted that she'd been struggling with both spirit attachments and dark entities, both in her home and in her aura, but they weren't there now. By holding one of Kelly's belongings I was able to scan her home remotely. Once I was energetically linked in I began the healing process by releasing a few of the spirits. They weren't bad by any means. They'd simply become a little lost and confused on their transition from their earthly lives to continue their existence in the dimensions of spirit world.

Her home was now clear, but still I sensed that something wasn't right. She went on her way and I vowed that from now on I'd always trust my gut! I pondered on what an important lesson I'd learned. By ignoring my instincts I'd caused a lot of additional work for myself. It takes a lot of time and energy to perform such a cleansing process. I'd never go against my instincts again.

At the end of the evening, I slumped into the armchair, finally about to relax, when I remembered the photo that Holy Amethyst had told me to take. I zoomed in on the picture I'd taken on my phone and an ice-cold chill reverberated through my bones. Sat there as plain as day were three ugly, distorted faces in the back of Kelly's car!

The Violet Flame shield had worked. Knowing that they couldn't penetrate the wall of fire without receiving the love of the angels, they'd decided to wait for her outside. What a lucky escape I'd had! I would only have agreed to perform a healing of that scale in the client's own home; otherwise it would mean clearing both their home and mine – double the work!

I've used the Violet Flame under the guidance of Holy Amethyst many times and you can use it, too. You don't need to be a healer and nor do you need to be engaged in dramatic circumstances, like in my story. You can use it when your difficult relative comes to visit, or even when there's a grumpy teenager in the house! Any time there's a risk that your mood can become contaminated, call in Lady Amethyst and the powers of the violet flame.

Keeper of the Violet Flame

The Violet Flame is a transformational spiritual tool that can help you to uncover the magic within your soul. It can also be used to transcend all limitations and darkness.

Over recent years, the Violet Flame has been dubbed the 'Silver Violet Flame', 'Rainbow Violet Flame', 'Diamond Violet Flame' and so forth. The truth is, the core of the Violet Flame itself has remained, but as we've undergone many energetic upgrades, it's merged with other light rays. As we rapidly evolve, more of the uses of the sacred flame are revealed to us.

The current keepers of the flame are Holy Amethyst, Archangel Zadkiel, and the Ascended Masters St Germain and Lady Portia. At the time of writing, the current model of the flame has evolved from a simple cleansing tool to the addition of many 'new' features. The most recent version includes access to the latest available angelic light codes for your ascension, as well as energetic activations that reawaken junk DNA, turning you into a superhuman. Here is an invocation that you can repeat to activate the Violet Flame:

Violet Flame Decree

Lady Amethyst can initiate you into the energies of the Violet Flame and will teach you many of its uses. If you're undergoing any shadow work, then the flame can show you how seeds of fear were planted within your psyche, allowing you to root them out, clear them and finally replace them with the truth.

You can also use the flame to cleanse negativity, develop psychic awareness and make yourself invisible. Here's a decree to call in the supercharged version of the Diamond Violet Flame:

~ Say, 'Diamond Violet Flame, be with me this hour. Show me my truth. Show me my power. Holy Amethyst, Holy Light, awaken in me now. Goddess given sight, keep me pure day and night.'

~ To make yourself invisible – one of the uses of the flame – simply call in Lady Amethyst and ask her to place the Violet Flame cloak over you.

~ Imagine her placing the hood over your head and fastening it securely around you.

~ Have a play with it.

~ Activate the cloak when you spot someone you know when you're out and about.

~ See whether or not they notice you!

~ Just remember to take it off again when you've finished.

I learned this the hard way when I was driving and three cars pulled out on me in one day. You definitely want to be seen when you're driving!

You can also place the cloak over a loved one – perhaps if a child is being bullied in school and you want to draw attention away from them. You can do this by asking Holy Amethyst the following:

'Holy Amethyst, under the Law of Grace, I ask that you place [name] under the violet cloak of invisibility to [reason, e.g., keep away bullies], if it's of the highest good of all. Thank you. Amen.'

Angel of Psychic Awareness

Lady Amethyst is a great teacher to work with if you'd like to develop your psychic clairs. She's the remover of psychic veils and will finely tune your sixth sense perceptions. Psychic development should be practised under the guidance of someone who has excellent abilities themselves, or with Lady Amethyst herself.

It's easy to blow a psychic gasket when practising alone. Not all of us have access to psychic tutors, but Holy Amethyst is the perfect companion with whom to embark upon this learning journey. She's available any time, any place. She'll open up your psychic awareness at a pace that's perfect for you. She says that a gradual awakening is much easier for the brain to handle, preventing data overload and making this additional information easier to process. Steady and slow ensures that you fully integrate your gifts and maintain a good sense of balance as you walk between worlds.

Holy Amethyst will communicate with your spirit guide team to assist you with your development. She'll also ensure that they convey accurate messages to you, perhaps with a little tweaking of your Third Eye chakra!

If you have yet to meet your gatekeeper guide – think the boss who's been with you since birth – then Lady Amethyst can facilitate this for you. A sound relationship with your gatekeeper guide is an excellent ally to have. In fact, once you become friends, you may wonder how you ever got on before without them!

It's important to note that angels and the spirit world vibrate on very different frequencies. For this reason, not all mediums can speak to angels and not all angel whisperers can receive spirit. The angelic kingdom is very high vibrational. Communicating with them means that you must elevate your consciousness through meditation, the ability to quiet the mind and by having very pure intentions. Working with spirit means that you're communicating with beings on the astral plane. While I'm all for psychic development, it's naïve to think that all beings who reside on this realm can be trusted.

They can't. Think humans without bodies – some people are nice, some not so nice. That's why you must take extra-special care when working with the spirit world and always use your psychic protection. Remain attentive and calm when working on this realm; after all, it's likely that you already astral travel most nights! Just remember the moth-to-the-flame analogy: the brighter your spiritual light shines, the more moths are attracted to the flame.

This is where Lady Amethyst comes in handy once again with the Violet Flame. She can make you invisible to low-frequency energy forms. If you're an energy healer or shamanic practitioner, then wearing the Violet Flame cloak allows you to travel through realms without being noticed. It'll also double as a shield when you're entering dense energy swamps, preventing negativity from piercing your aura.

The Violet Duo

Holy Amethyst's twin flame is Archangel Zadkiel. Together, they hold the frequencies of the seventh ray of Divine alchemy and transmutation. They're also the keepers of the diamond violet light codes – a facet of the higher angelic heart, which enables you to receive energetic upgrades with higher-vibrational ascension codes.

This beautiful duo are a sight for sore eyes. The ethereal hues of violet that surround them both are absolutely mesmerizing.

Their etheric portal, the Temple of Purity, is located in the mountains of Cuba in the Caribbean.

Archangel Zadkiel

Archangel Zadkiel's name translates to 'Righteousness of God'. He helps people to make good choices and the right decisions. He's very fair and just. He appears to me with a brown beard and golden-brown short hair. He wears a crisp-white tunic with a deep-purple sleeveless jacket over the top. He wears a chunky, beaded amethyst necklace that has a large pendant on it in the shape of an eight-pointed cross.

Archangel Zadkiel will encourage you to remain distant from temptations of the sensory pleasures including sex, food, alcohol or anything in excess. He reminds us that it's healthy to have treats, but overconsuming and overindulging comes from a desire of the ego, not the soul. We confirm this to ourselves when we later regret eating that extra cream cake, or buying that designer bed linen that we couldn't really afford.

He can help you to transcend desires of the body if you feel that you're being controlled by the egotistical mind. Excellent news if you're about to give up caffeine or go on one too many shopping splurges, as Archangel Zadkiel will give you the power to say no.

Archangel Zadkiel is one of the angels of justice and freedom. He can be called upon to support you in court, when you have a dispute or when you're having a meeting of any kind with officials. He'll ensure that you're fairly treated and that justice is served.

He's also a member of the Karmic Board, which means he oversees the Hall of Records and has direct access to personal, ancestral and planetary karma. Together with Holy Amethyst, the Karmic Board can help you to break free from samsara (karmic cycles). You can call upon either of these angels to grant you permission to view your soul contracts.

Working with Holy Amethyst

Before you meet Lady Amethyst, next is a list of crystals that can help you to tune in to her frequency. She also resonates with the powerful, cleansing herb of rosemary and the colour purple. If you have time, perhaps you'd like to make a mini altar in her honour. You could lay down a purple cloth, light a white candle and burn rosemary essential oil. You could even place one of her crystals in your hand or on the altar and sit in a silent meditative state in front of it. These additional steps can amplify your receptivity to receiving her wisdom.

Holy Amethyst's Gemstones

The following crystals have the healing vibrations that resonate with the work of Lady Amethyst:

- amethyst

- lapis lazuli

- Herkimer diamond

- lavender agate

- spirit quartz

- fluorite

Holding or wearing any of the listed crystals will serve as a reminder of any intentions that you're working through with Lady Amethyst. They'll also raise your vibration to her energetic frequency.

INVOCATION: CALLING IN HOLY AMETHYST

Now that you have an understanding of Lady Amethyst's attributes, you're ready to get stuck in and meet her for yourself.

You will need:

~ a white candle

~ matches

~ a pen and a piece of paper

~ a bundle of cleansing herbs for burning

When you're ready to call in Holy Amethyst, carefully light the herb bundle and pass the smoke through your aura to create a sacred space. Sit in peace and relax. Take a few deep, calming breaths to centre yourself before you begin:

~ Place your hands into the prayer position, gently level with your Heart chakra.

~ Call in Holy Amethyst by whispering her name three times.

~ Say, 'Holy Amethyst, Holy Amethyst, Holy Amethyst.'

~ Light the white candle.

~ State the following invocation: 'She who is Holy I call forth to complete me. I am pure, I am whole, I am Holy Amethyst. She, who is the keeper of the sacred Flame of Transmutation, I call forth to dispel all illusions and darkness both within and without me. I am pure, I am whole, I am Holy Amethyst. She who sees all, remover of veils, I call forth to remove all perceived obstacles and blockages of my inner vision. I am clairvoyant, I am pure, I am whole, I am Holy Amethyst. And so it is.'

~ Visualize or feel her loving energy growing in the room.

~ She comes towards you and steps into your aura.

~ Allow her to fill you with her sacred violet light.

~ Perhaps Holy Amethyst reveals a message to you now.

~ Spend some time in meditation to absorb her wisdom.

~ Be sure to take notes afterwards – the information you gathered may prove useful later.

~ Say a big heartfelt 'thank you' to Holy Amethyst.

LIFTING THE VEIL OF THE THIRD EYE

Next is an exercise that you can use to unlock your clairvoyance with a blessing from Lady Amethyst.

You will need:

~ a small amethyst crystal

~ a pen and paper for journalling afterwards

~ a dried herb bundle for burning

Cleanse your aura with the herb smoke to clear and uplift your energy and then practise some deep breathing to raise your vibration before you begin:

~ When you're ready, lie down somewhere comfortable.

~ Call in Lady Amethyst by reciting her invocation (previous exercise) or by stating her name three times.

~ Place your amethyst crystal on the centre of your brow, allowing it to rest here throughout the exercise – this will gently stimulate your Third Eye chakra.

~ Place your awareness on the crystal in the centre of your brow while breathing deeply.

~ Once you begin to feel the forehead tingling, visualize the petals of a deep purple rose slowly opening, increasing your psychic sensitivity to the angels petal by petal.

~ In the centre of the flower, you see a stone archway.

~ A long lilac veil drapes across the entrance, dancing and waving to a gentle breeze.

~ Gently lifting the veil of perception to one side, you walk through the stone entrance.

~ Inside, the cool walls made of amethyst crystal are shimmering.

~ You notice Holy Amethyst and Archangel Zadkiel stood either side of a grand fireplace.

~ Large violet flames jump and flicker in the fire.

~ You make your way towards it.

~ Holy Amethyst is holding a golden sceptre with a candle at one end.

~ She points it towards the fire and lights the wick on the roaring flames.

~ She turns to you and asks if you're ready to see beyond the veil of illusion and separation.

~ Next, she takes the sceptre and holds the candle up to your Third Eye chakra.

~ She gently ignites a small Violet Flame within your brow.

~ The flame burns away barriers and blockages, along with veils of judgement, fear and misconception.

~ Witness the purification of your vision.

~ Tap in to feelings of peace and happiness.

~ Now that you're totally clear, you'll find it easier to stick to the best pathway ahead.

~ Take as long as you need to complete this process.

~ When you're ready, the angels stand beside you ready to walk you back.

~ As you exit the stone archway, you tear down the flowing curtain and hand it to Holy Amethyst for disposal.

~ She places a white sacred symbol of your choice over the doorway to keep it pure.

~ Thank her by holding your hands over your Heart chakra and simply whisper thank you three times.

~ Close the rose petals of the Third Eye chakra until your next journey.

~ Bring your awareness back into the room by wiggling your fingers and toes.

~ Take a deep breath in through your nose and exhale through the mouth while making an 'ahhh' sound.

Remove the crystal from your forehead and store it in a small pouch or piece of cloth. This will help to contain the high-vibrational energies that are now stored within it. You can use the stone again when you practice developing your clairs.

Remember to take notes – even if it seems insignificant, get it all down, as it may make sense in the future. And always get some fresh air and have a light snack to ground your energy.

It's common to experience light headaches when developing the Third Eye chakra. If this happens to you, go through the exercise a bit slower. Remember that you're always in control of your awakening process. If the energy seems too intense, ask the angels to turn the vibration down. They'll always accommodate you, ensuring that you have a pleasant experience. If you're already psychically 'seeing' and want to lessen the visions, then in this exercise imagine placing a veil up over the Third Eye chakra. Or even better, imagine it as a solid door closing – you can even lock it. This exercise has worked a treat on the rare occasions that clients have wanted me to close down their psychic gifts.

With practice, you'll master turning the psychic visions on and off. If I'm switched off, it's rare I'll see. This is how I maintain balance between worlds. Keeping them separate keeps me whole. You need to keep in touch with the Earth reality.

The following exercise is fabulous for cleansing ancestral karma. In this instance I'll be using it to clear illness that runs in families, but you can use it to clear inherited beliefs, traumas, fears or whatever you like. This is what's so exciting about working with the ancient feminine ways – there are no hard and fast rules and there's no manual or guidebook. The secrets of the Divine feminine come from an internal force rather than an external one. It's inherent within you. You're free to get totally creative.

KARMA CLEANSE

Before you begin, have a good think about obvious things that run in your family. For example, all of the women on my mother's side of the family have suffered from varicose veins after pregnancy. Not me, though – I'm the exception. However, it's down to more than luck, diet or the gym! I made the conscious decision many years ago that I remain free from inheriting any of the illnesses or diseases that ran in the family and I've simply avoided them as a result.

Some people make themselves sick – inadvertently, of course – by assuming that they'll develop an illness because it's in their genes. Quantum physics proves that we become what we focus upon (and what we focus upon is influenced by our observation). If we believe that we'll develop cancer as everyone else in the family suffered from it, then it's very likely that that's exactly what we'll manifest. But let me go a level deeper. What about those who are mindful about their thoughts, who eat alkaline foods, who use the Law of Attraction? What about when they still get sick?

I asked Holy Amethyst this very question and one day, when I was with a cancer patient, she showed me what had occurred within this client that had allowed this disease to manifest to such a mindful yogi. Unknowingly, she'd carried the energetic frequency of the illness in her DNA, passed down from previous generations. The good news is we can act before we've inherited sickness from our ancestors. We can use the flame right away to heal the line. Here's how:

Ancestral Healing: Activate the Violet Strand DNA

When you're ready to call in Holy Amethyst, set up a sacred space by burning incense and candles.

You will need:

~ incense

~ candles

~ matches

~ a pen and a piece of paper

Relax in a place where you can remain peaceful and quiet for at least 20 minutes:

~ Take some deep belly breaths and starting from your toes, working your way up to your head, gently relax all of your muscles one by one.

~ Call in Holy Amethyst by singing or whispering her name three times.

~ Say, 'Holy Amethyst, Holy Amethyst, Holy Amethyst.'

~ Visualize her violet aura wrapping around you, offering you both healing and protection.

~ Bring your awareness to your pineal gland, a tiny pine cone in the centre of your brain.

~ Holding your attention here, chant 'Om' seven times.

~ Allow Holy Amethyst to seal in a blessing by kissing your pineal gland gently.

~ As she does so, it opens clean in half.

~ Inside, you see beautifully carved wooden shelves with thousands upon thousands of books sat upon them.

~ A large black book catches your eye on the left-hand side of the room.

~ Visualize taking the book into your hands.

~ Press it close to your Heart chakra for a second to connect to its intelligence.

~ You open it up and inside the pages reveal all of the unproductive energy imprints that you've inherited from your ancestors on your mother's side.

~ Spend a few minutes taking in what you've discovered.

~ Tear a page from the book and place it into Holy Amethyst's open palms, which are ablaze with the violet flame of transmutation.

~ You immediately feel lighter as the page curls and shrinks as it's destroyed.

~ Hear the paper crackle and burn.

~ Feel the warmth of the flame caressing your skin.

~ Visualize family members of this line becoming free from the shackles of their past.

~ Take three deep breaths in through the nose and out through the mouth.

~ The power of your breath activates the pineal gland.

~ You watch blissfully as an energetic DNA ladder emerges from the pineal gland and structures itself throughout your chakra system below.

~ Holy Amethyst blows a warm violet mist upon your brow and a Violet Flame ignites within your Third Eye chakra.

~ The glow of the flame brightens and a stream of light cascades through your DNA ladder.

~ The light ripples out into every cell in your body, transforming and healing your feminine ancestral line.

~ Take a deep breath in through the nose and out through the mouth.

~ Take your awareness back into the Hall of Records.

~ You now notice a huge golden book over on the right-hand side of the room.

~ You pick it up and taking a deep breath in, you inhale the smell of the ink on the old parchment.

~ This magical book contains all of the karmic records of your past, present and potential future.

~ Flicking through the book, you see photographs and information about the lives of all of your relatives on your father's side of the family.

~ The final page reveals unproductive manifestations that you've inherited from your masculine ancestral lineage.

~ You may or may not have been aware of them.

~ Tear this page from the big book.

~ As before with the feminine ancestral line, place the page into Holy Amethyst's open palms, which are ablaze with the violet flame of transmutation.

~ Watch the paper shrink away, along with negative traits, poor health and so on.

~ Visualize family members of this line becoming free from the shackles of their past.

~ Take three deep breaths in through the nose and out through the mouth.

~ Once again, focus upon the pineal gland and see or feel violet light cascading over your DNA ladder, transmuting patterns as it travels down, cleansing the chakras below.

~ Free from diseases, unhelpful mindsets and fears, you're now a pure vessel, untarnished, to protect the future generations who follow – no more diseases, no more negative mindsets, no more fears are to be carried through to the generations of the future with you as the vessel.

~ All you will now carry through to the generations in the future is love, good qualities and strengths.

~ When you feel ready, open your eyes.

~ Physically enjoy the sensation of your body and how it feels right at this moment, now you've cleared everything, to help you to return to the here and now; then proceed with the next step.

~ Taking the pen and paper, at the top of the page, write the following: 'I [your name] hereby declare that from this day forth, I am free from all influences upon my energy. I am sovereign in mind, body and soul. I have the power to clear energetic threads linking me to people and places of past, present and future, and so it is.'

~ Sign your name.

~ Take a deep breath and read the statement aloud three times to seal in your fully healed DNA (strands).

~ The high-vibrational energy from Lady Amethyst is likely to have awakened your chakras, so visualize them closing down one by one (like the petals of a flower).

~ Give thanks to Holy Amethyst and your ancestors by stating 'Holy Amethyst, Ancestors, thank you for this opportunity for healing, and so it is.'

~ Touch the floor with your hands, reconnecting your energy back to Earth.

~ You may like to have a hot drink and take notes of your experience.

~ You can choose whether or not you'd like to keep hold of your declaration, or you could burn it. If you choose the latter, set the intention that when you do, the rising smoke sends your declaration to heaven.

Being proactive by cultivating better health and more happiness while having a sense of living on purpose (with intention) is the way forwards in the new age of the feminine. There are finally enough of us spiritually evolved and in the process of reinstating our powers that it's at last acceptable, in fact necessary, for us to manifest a fabulous life filled with all of the joys imaginable. It's time for our dreams to become reality.

~

The exercises in this chapter are very advanced practices. Take your time going through them and only practise them when you feel ready. You can always ask Holy Amethyst for a sign if you're unsure. Within the next 24 hours, you may hear SpongeBob SquarePants on the TV singing 'I'm Ready, Promotion', which would be a clear yes. Or you may see a road sign that says 'Road ahead closed', which would mean not just yet. You can really only succeed with her by your side.

CHAPTER 3

Lady Aurora
Dawn of the Goddess

The radiant Archeia Aurora is an angel of 'God's light'. Her Latin name translates to 'Dawn', which suits her perfectly, as her presence immediately uplifts you so you can see the sunnier side of life. She assures you that no matter how long or dark the night may have been, a new day awaits you, making her a great ally when you're feeling that all is lost.

Lady Aurora will help you to rise from the ashes and step into your personal power, and encourage you to shine your light, just like you're meant to. By helping us to trust our gut and use the power of discernment, Lady Aurora is especially helpful to empaths. Her light will dispel any confusion caused by external influences upon your energy, enabling you to recognize when you've absorbed emotions that belong to another person.

Lady Aurora's Appearance

Lady Aurora appears to me with gentle deep brown eyes and she's always wearing a beautiful wide smile. Adorned in a ruby-red satin gown, big golden curls trail down her back. She has the most amazing crystalline wings that span out like glistening rays of the sun. Her aura may appear to be bright gold in colour. At other times, you may notice additional waves of light dancing both through and around her, similar to the Northern Lights (aurora borealis).

She emanates yellows and golds to enlighten, empower and energize you. And blues, greens and purples to clear your energetic slate and rebalance your energy bodies, with reds and oranges to ignite sparks of passion and drive within you.

Lady Aurora's Energy

Archeia Aurora has a very recognizable energy. When in her presence a feeling of deep peace overcomes you. Unruly thinking is instantly replaced with clarity.

She represents The Ace of Swords in the Tarot deck. This is the card of resurrection, epiphanies and conquering your thinking. Lady Aurora reminds us that just like in the message of this card, all of our struggles, pain and suffering were meaningful and played a crucial role in the forging of our spirits, making us who we are today.

She's the archetypal innocent child who's untainted, free from the projections and opinions of others (elders, parents or teachers). Children have confidence in voicing their needs or opinions. We all know about it when a baby is uncomfortable! She encourages you to be the same. Be honest about what you want, be yourself and heal or let go of whatever may be disturbing your peace.

She can help you with:

• developing your personal power

• enhancing your intuition and gut feeling

• taking back your power

- developing clairsentience
- protecting clairempathy
- facilitating a rebirth
- new beginnings
- igniting passion
- developing strength
- summoning courage
- living in a state of authenticity
- raising ambition
- growing self-esteem
- radiating self-confidence
- maintaining integrity
- healing your Solar Plexus chakra
- establishing clear thinking
- finding answers
- developing inner peace

Lady Aurora's Calling Cards

Here's a list of Archeia Aurora's calling cards for you to look out for. If you notice any of her personal tokens that are listed, you can take it as confirmation that she wants to work with you or she's trying to get your attention:

- Lady Aurora's number sequence is 555. You may repeatedly see various formations of this number including 5, 55, 555, 5555 and so forth.

- The number 5 denotes coming into your personal power, freedom, challenges and change.

- Lady Aurora's animal totem is the phoenix. And after starting to work with her, you may notice images of the phoenix in odd places, like on the side of a van – further signs that this Archangel is around you.

- Your Solar Plexus chakra may tingle and feel warm.

- You may suddenly make sense of a situation that had been troubling you. Epiphanies and answers seemingly just come to light.

- You may feel inspired to start a new project, or make a long-needed change. Synchronicities will occur to inspire you further.

- She may make your candle flicker during meditation when the room is breeze-free.

- You may see images of the sun or rainbows on children's clothing, on a bus ticket or on an oracle card.

- You may capture the sun's rays on photos by 'accident'.

- Her flowers are sunflowers (liberation) and snowdrops (new beginnings).

Angel of Resurrection

They say that the darkest hour is just before dawn, meaning that stressful situations can feel as though they get worse just before they're about to get better. This peak in darkness is a pivotal point of change, because there's only one way to go when you hit rock bottom – and that's upwards. Lady Aurora is that very dawn. She's the light who comes to our aid and guides us safely back into the light. She inspires us to give that final push, walk the extra mile and above all, maintain a feeling of hope.

Lady Aurora can be called upon to help you to face any area of your life that needs transforming. Along with other Archangels, she oversees a spiritual process that all human beings endure on their ascension journey: the Spiritual Death. A spiritual death can occur several times in one's lifetime. Relax, it doesn't mean that you have to die or have a near-death experience to undergo it! You can think of it as a process that allows part of our ego and false self to die so we can be reborn anew, free from shackles of the past.

You've probably experienced a Dark Night of the Soul already. Perhaps the breakdown of a relationship, the death of a loved one, or any other kind of loss that may have propelled you into a downward spiral towards an all-time low. In the game of life, it's possible and maybe even inevitable that you'll endure this process again. This is what Lady Aurora has to say about this:

Beloved ones, your lifetimes on Earth bring you experiences in which you will endure great emotional pain and suffering. But let me reassure you – I am here for every single person, every step of the way. Call upon me. I will provide a beacon of light to guide you home when you are lost and I will ignite the flame of will within your soul, to strengthen you to see another day.

Human life experiences can be harsh at times, but remember: there is always an opportunity for growth. A glimmer of light emerges from the cracks of a broken heart that has been struck by grief. As surely as the sun sets each evening, it will surely rise again each morning. All things pass. I will restore your faith and help you to find peace.

Lady Aurora's presence is a welcome relief in times of uncertainty. When we lack clarity, we can be left feeling as though we're fumbling around in the dark. Lady Aurora wants all of us to be at peace in our lives.

She can help you to turn chaos into calm by showing you the way forwards. She guides you towards the light at the end of the tunnel and helps you to rebuild your life after turmoil. She provides you with insight so that you learn from your experiences and ensure that your future is assembled on solid foundations.

Just remember that under the Law of Free Will, you must ask an angel to help you. They can never intervene unless your soul sends out an SOS.

Angel Encounter

I was first introduced to Archeia Aurora when I was about 20 years old. I was a self-employed holistic therapist at the time and was working one day per week at a mental health outpatients' clinic. I loved giving treatments and helping to inspire people to heal their lives, like I had. But I'd begun to notice a pattern.

Each week during and after that particular day's work, I'd begin to feel unwell. The symptoms that occurred included feeling energetically drained and slightly anxious with a splitting headache. I knew that this wasn't right. I arrived home that evening, flopped on the bed and slapped a cold compress across my forehead. My eyes heavy, I asked my guardian angel to shed some light on the situation. Why did I feel ill whenever I worked at this place?

Inhaling the sweet scent of the lavender oil from the dripping wet flannel, I found that I couldn't keep myself awake and dozed off almost straight away.

The next thing I knew, I was stood outside an ethereal golden castle. Hung in the sky above the castle was a huge rainbow-coloured orb, slowly rotating and shining rays of light.

Flitting around me smiling were about a dozen small angels, each about 1 metre (3 feet) in height, joyfully beckoning me inside. Trusting them completely, I felt compelled to follow them. Inside the circular entrance, I paused to admire the sacred geometric symbols finely carved into the high walls and archways.

A vast curtain of flowers cascaded from a stained-glass window, which displayed the image of a yellow rose encapsulated within a glorious orange rising sun. I could hear a melody of soft voices singing. It was so beautiful. The enchantingly sweet lull of music sent ripples of electrical currents throughout my body. I felt intoxicated with an indescribable sense of relaxation and warmth in my heart. My arms outstretched, I gazed up to the open-air ceiling and mouthed 'Thank you.' I knew that I was in a very special place receiving a deep spiritual healing.

In this lucid dream, I wondered where in the universe I was 'visiting'. The penny dropped when I recognized a familiar face entering the room. It was Archangel Uriel. I knew then that I was at his etheric retreat over the Tatra Mountains, on the border of Poland and Slovakia.

'There is someone who you need to meet,' Archangel Uriel impressed in my mind.

'Who?' I cried in anticipation.

A shimmering beam of light descended from the orb in the sky and into the room. Stopping right in front of me, a dazzling female silhouette emerged from the light.

I instantly dropped to my knees in reverence. For the first time – or at least the first time I could remember – I was in the presence of the breathtakingly beautiful angel Lady Aurora, Archangel Uriel's twin ray.

I'll always remember how she made me feel: absolute bliss and carefree – her peaceful presence was a soothing balm for my spirit.

As she cupped my chin in her hands, Lady Aurora's loving brown eyes met mine, her gentle gaze relaxing me all the more deeply. While maintaining eye contact, she moved her hands and rested them gently over my abdomen. After a few moments, she proceeded to 'pull off' one of my energy bodies. It was a strange sensation but it was comfortable; it was as easy as removing an item of clothing.

She explained to me that I was an empath and the reason why I was feeling so unwell when giving treatments was because I wasn't shielding my energy sufficiently.

Holding up the energy body like an all-in-one suit, she pointed to the belly area. I could clearly see that it was clogged and dirty. Small masses of dark brown, smokelike energy knitted around my 'suit'. The stagnated ki (chi/life-force energy) stretched and pulled away at the intricate fabric that bound the body together, leaving it with tiny holes.

It was so fascinating to see the damage that I'd unknowingly done to myself. But what was even more interesting was the fact that I could also read this energy! I knew exactly whom it had belonged to and when I'd picked it up.

This was a real eye-opener for me. No wonder I'd been feeling so rough! I'd been collecting all of my clients' emotions and carrying them in my own aura. Pulling the energy body back over my head, Lady Aurora simply nodded when I asked her if she could help me to clear the blocked energy. A sunshine-like glow began to swell in her belly. Aligning her sun centre with mine, she proceeded to project a beam of light directly into my Solar Plexus centre. Tiny red-and-purple flames imploded here and there, as if they were extinguishing the stale energy that I'd accumulated.

The collection of negative energy was being banished. Some of it was mine and some of it had belonged to others. It was such a relief to release it. I immediately felt much lighter and clearer.

I asked Archeia Aurora whether sadness and suffering played an essential part in the spiritual awakening process. She confirmed, 'Yes, because only from the darkest night can you observe the most glorious of light.'

The alarm clock woke me and I leaped out of bed, disorientated. I'd slept for 16 hours! After writing my experience down in my diary, I put the pen down and smiled to myself. Meeting Lady Aurora had left me feeling like a new woman. I realized that it's fine to embrace your shadow. It didn't mean that I was a spiritual failure because I had fears or doubts. It was all part of being a human being.

I quickly became good friends with Lady Aurora and she went on to teach me many things, including how to prevent my empathic gifts from loading me with collective energy gunk.

Angel of Empaths

Archeia Aurora is currently working very closely with the growing number of empaths and healers who are incarnating upon this planet. She explained to me that while some souls are born with empathic gifts, many have developed their sensitivity later in life, either through their spiritual practice or simply in response to the rising vibrational frequency on Earth.

By working with her, she can help you to distinguish where you end and where another person begins in an energetic sense – a classic struggle for new-found sensitives who unknowingly have a tendency to pick up on everything.

Lady Aurora will let you know when your energy needs clearing or when it needs extra shielding from unavoidable encounters with negative people, high emotions, energy vampires or mood hoovers.

She explained to me that the key to making the most of having empathic gifts is ensuring that you clear your energy often and always trust your gut. Your gut, or Solar Plexus chakra, is the energy centre that 'reads' the space that you enter and occupy. Lady Aurora will light up your Solar Plexus chakra so that you're always aware and on form.

By meditating or calling upon Lady Aurora, you can fill up your energy tank whenever you feel as though you're becoming drained. She loves nothing more than sharing her endless supply of light.

Like all angels, all you need to do is ask and it's done. If you feel like you aren't holding the reins and are unable to control your gifts, Lady Aurora will teach you how to turn them on and off. She'll open up empathy in those who wish to develop this gift if you ask her to. If you're dealing with a particularly hard or difficult person, you can ask this Archeia to soften their heart, enabling them to become more compassionate and open.

ARE YOU AN EMPATH?

You may now be wondering if you, too, are an empath. I find that most people who are drawn to spirituality are empaths, as it frequently comes hand in hand. As your consciousness expands, so do your psychic gifts.

Here's a basic set of questions to help you to identify any extra-sensitive gifts that you may possess:

~ Can you not stand being around angry people?

~ Do you hate violent TV shows?

~ Do crowds and loud places make you feel uneasy?

~ Do you feel sympathy pains for others?

~ Are you very intuitive?

~ Do you prefer your own company?

~ Can you 'see right through people'?

~ Does cruelty to animals or polluting the planet make you feel physically ill?

If you've answered yes to more than three of these questions, then it's likely that you're an empath. In which case you'll benefit dramatically from working with this Archeia.

Angel of Peace

Lady Aurora is an angel of the sixth ray, the ruby ray of peace. Part of her mission is to help humanity to establish heaven on Earth – to find peace.

She reassures all of those suffering from busy minds and uncertain hearts that harmony is more easily restored when you have a team of angels rooting for you. A problem shared?

Lady Aurora explains that you don't need to try to save the world or change anybody to bring about world peace. She says that if enough individuals work on leading a harmonious lifestyle and live by example then that'll be enough to create a knock-on effect upon those around us. People will feel your bliss emanating from you. They'll want to know what your secret is. Therefore, you can stay just as you are without having to do anything. Peace is an inside job, attained through mindfulness and meditation.

Lady Aurora also adds that we can't always remain at peace all of the time and that's okay. If a stressful situation is unfolding around you and you're finding it impossible to control your emotions, then ask her team of ruby ray angels to sing songs of tranquillity above your abode.

Angel of Empowerment

Lady Aurora helps to empower individuals to speak their truth. She says that being honest to both yourself and others is a crucial aspect of attaining lasting peace within ourselves. She'll use her fiery energies to give you a swift boost of self-confidence, encouraging you to live the life that you truly desire.

In the past, it was unsafe for women to express their true nature – and it still is in some countries. For centuries we've hidden our interests, gifts and talents to avoid judgement and persecution, but that era is swiftly coming to a close. As the feminine and masculine fall into balance, our time is now.

Lady Aurora understands how it feels to have sold yourself short. It becomes second nature to most women to put other people's needs before your own, but she tells you from the bottom of her heart that you should never settle for less or compromise yourself too much. She'll help you to become accustomed to placing yourself higher up on your priority list.

We all know that you can't pour from an empty cup and so you must fill it regularly by doing what you love. This will help you to sustain balance, health and happiness, as well as enable you to give love to others.

The Blazing Duo

Lady Aurora's twin flame is the mighty Archangel Uriel. He's one of my all-time favourite Archangels. I love his energy so much; he just lights me up inside.

Archangel Uriel

Archangel Uriel's name translates to 'Fire of God'. He's the great angel who illuminates you with the wisdom and truth streamed directly from the mind of God. When he visits me, Archangel Uriel wears red and gold Eastern-looking robes. He's quite handsome with short chestnut brown hair and a short, neat beard.

He's a jolly angel with a great sense of humour. I find that when I've been working with him, I naturally become very witty myself. The synchronicities that Archangel Uriel brings to you will more than likely make you laugh. His confirmations come in the form of cartoons or jokes and can be really hilarious.

I was giving a psychic reading to a very depressed client one day. She was on the verge of tears, when Archangel Uriel burst into the room laughing deliriously, wearing a pair of green wellies. He told me to ask her about the green wellies. I couldn't help but laugh and even though it seemed a bit nutty, I still shared the scene with her. She immediately erupted with laughter and confirmed that she'd been doing the gardening in her late father's green wellies that weekend. Even though they were four sizes too big, she didn't have the heart to throw them away.

The evidence brought her much-needed comfort and reassurance that she's still being watched over. The whole mood was lifted through Archangel Uriel's ability to bring humour to the situation. He says that laughter releases natural endorphins within the body, making us feel contented and at peace.

He's often depicted holding a lantern or a flame. This is very symbolic and holds several meanings. The flame represents how Archangel Uriel will help you to make an informed decision. Being the angel of crossroads, he'll unburden you of doubt. If you're in two minds, lack clarity and generally feel stuck you can invoke his sacred flame to clear your mind and become decisive.

Archangel Uriel also helps us to focus our attention on the task at hand, making him a great angel to work with if you're studying. He provides ideas and creative inspiration to artists and writers; he has a truly brilliant mind. When Archangel Uriel comes to you with his lantern, he's telling you that the answers that you seek lie within. He's encouraging you to be your own guru, and to meditate and connect to the mind of Source yourself. He believes in you and so should you.

Archangel Uriel and Lady Aurora make a great team. The feminine energies of Lady Aurora will awaken inspiration within you and the complementary energy of Archangel Uriel will ensure that you stay committed to your goal. Their energies are felt on Earth most strongly on a Thursday (Thor's day), which corresponds to the planet Jupiter, signifying expansion, confidence, action, luck and enthusiasm.

Working with Lady Aurora

After reading the earlier sections and learning the basics about Lady Aurora, you may now feel inclined to work with her. Perhaps you've noticed some of her calling cards already… Whether you're ready to reinvent yourself, have discovered that you're an empath, or you simply want to gain inspiration and insight, you'll want to meet her for yourself.

Before you invoke her into your rituals and the exercises that follow, you may choose to set up an altar dedicated to her. If so, use lovely golden-yellow candles and a yellow altar cloth, and try to obtain some copal resin or dragon's blood for burning.

You can also wear or hold any of the following crystals that are strongly aligned with her energetic frequency:

Lady Aurora's Gemstones

The following crystals have the healing vibrations that resonate with the work of Lady Aurora:

- heliodor
- fire opal
- citrine
- yellow calcite

Wear or hold any of these gemstones to enhance your sensitivity to Lady Aurora's energy.

You can use this next mini ritual to introduce yourself to the wonderful healing presence of Lady Aurora. Connecting to her energy will help you to stay true to yourself, sharpen your intuition and clear out old energy from your consciousness. It can also be useful to do this ritual when you need a burst of inspiration or are feeling emotionally beaten.

 INVOCATION: CALLING IN LADY AURORA

For this exercise, you'll only need a few 'magical tools':

~ a yellow candle and matches

~ dragon's blood resin and charcoal disc for burning

~ a pen and some paper in case you receive direct messages or symbols from Lady Aurora after this exercise

These items are optional. They'll help you to tune in to the vibration of Lady Aurora and the cleansing element of Fire.

Light the candle and burn a pinch of the dragon's blood resin to initiate the start of the invocation, then you can begin:

~ Gently placing your hands into the prayer position on your Heart chakra, say aloud, 'Lady Aurora, Lady Aurora, Lady Aurora,' to invite her presence into your space.

~ Focus on breathing in through the nose and out through the mouth slowly and deeply for five breaths.

~ Imagine Lady Aurora stood in front of you now.

~ Say, 'Archeia Aurora, thank you for igniting my sacred flame of light. Help me to be at peace while all falseness is revealed and stripped away from me. I walk away easily from all beliefs, situations, people and places that hold me back from living in harmony and integrity. I am free to walk the path of my dreams. I am safe to shine my light into the world. I understand that I am the resurrection and the light of my life. I am the dawn of my new day. Thank you for walking beside me as I transform into the best version of me. And so it is.'

~ Feel her warm, peaceful energy engulfing you, gently raising your vibration.

~ Take as long as you like to bask in her light.

~ Feel free to ask her about your personal requests, as she may be able to offer guidance.

~ Take a deep breath in and out.

~ Write Lady Aurora at the top of the page on your sheet of paper and without thinking, just write or draw any messages that come to mind.

~ Channel information directly from her now.

~ Trust whatever it is that's revealed to you right now.

~ Now, imagine that the information was for someone else (because that's easier).

~ How would you interpret any symbols or messages that you received?

~ When you're ready, take a deep breath in and, smiling, say, 'Thank you.'

~ Stretch your body, coming back into ordinary reality.

~ Blow out your candle.

After making this connection with Lady Aurora, you'll have attuned yourself to having a deeper perception of her presence. You can use the same exercise to channel messages from any angel you wish. Taking notes of your experience is a good habit to enforce. When you look back at the messages, in time you'll come to know what they meant. This will help you tremendously in decoding channelled messages in future, in addition to instilling in you more trust in your developing divination skills.

As Lady Aurora governs the Solar Plexus chakra, she's the perfect angel to call in to help you to release any trapped emotions in your aura that have latched on to you via this chakra gate. Any hankering negative emotions locked in here may belong to you, or you may have collected them in your energy field when interacting with others. Here's a fabulous exercise that you can use to clear your energy body – Lady Aurora taught it to me herself:

CLEAR YOUR EMOTIONAL BODY

I go through this quick process after every psychic reading that I give. You may wish to practise it if you've had a hard day or offered someone a shoulder to cry on. This will ensure that you clear and let go of any unwanted energy that you may have absorbed.

~ Call in Lady Aurora by placing your hands into prayer posture and say, 'Lady Aurora, Lady Aurora, Lady Aurora.'

~ Feel her loving presence enter the room.

~ She stands directly in front of you.

~ A glistening golden light emanates from her open palms.

~ Using the power of your breath, begin to draw her pure angelic healing energy in through your nose.

~ Her warm light gradually fills your entire body.

~ Now, imagine that you're filling up with so much light that it begins to escape through your pores and starts to shine out of you.

~ The shining light illuminates your energy body (aura), allowing you to scan it.

~ Observe any marks, lumps, holes, hooks or other attachments.

~ To remove any clogged energy that you may have detected, use your breath to release it by simply exhaling a grey or black fog through your mouth.

~ Repeat this cycle of taking in golden light and breathing out dark smoke several times until you 'see' in your mind's eye that you're breathing out golden light and your body is clear.

~ Now, in your mind, ask Lady Aurora to call in her fire dragons.

~ These gentle giants surround you, facing you from each direction – in front, behind, above, below, and to the right and left of you.

~ Lady Aurora gives them the nod and they simultaneously breathe a warm, cleansing fire over you, covering you from head to toe.

~ Relax as the energetic flame soothes both your body and aura.

~ Finally, allow them to extend into the room you're occupying, consuming any negativity in the vicinity.

~ When the process is complete, stroke the dragons and thank them.

~ Ask Lady Aurora to sew together any holes in your aura (if you found any).

~ Visualize your aura as strong and sturdy.

~ Give thanks to Lady Aurora.

~ Wash your hands and splash your face to use the power of water to ground your energies to the here and now.

~ If you still feel a little spaced out, have a bite to eat or inhale some essential oils such as peppermint or rosemary.

This wonderful exercise is quick and easy once you're familiar with the instructions that Lady Aurora has provided. You'll really notice a difference in your vitality if you practise this exercise regularly. It'll keep your personal energy safe from psychic attack and even boost your immune system, because all disease enters the body through damage to energy and emotional bodies (layers of the auric field surrounding your body).

Now that your energy field is clear and well-housed, you may wish to accelerate your spiritual gifts by uploading light codes from our sun. The great ancient civilizations understood the importance of the sun and some cultures even worshipped it. There are many solar temples dotted across the planet, such as Stonehenge in Wiltshire. This is where they'd observe the movement of the sun and tune in to its life-giving energy force. The Grand Central Sun is a Star Gate that broadcasts high-vibrational light to our planet, using our sun as a filter. If you're feeling ready for some ascension upgrades, do try this exercise under the guidance and care of Lady Aurora. Here's how:

The Grand Central Sun

Lady Aurora can increase your spiritual awareness and enhance your intuitive gifts by granting you more access to light codes from the Grand Central Sun.

Activation codes are imparted upon Earth every single day through our own sun, which transmits them directly from the Grand Central Sun portal. When we open ourselves up to receiving more light, unused parts of our brain and junk DNA begin to awaken, accelerating our evolution on all levels. You don't need Lady Aurora to receive light codes – they're available to everyone. However, with her help you can be more direct. She'll source the specific activation codes for whatever it is you're trying to evolve, awaken or enhance.

Think of her as having your very own tour guide in a foreign land. You can enjoy being in a beautiful place, but you have yet to learn all the history or the best things to see. Lady Aurora will uncover all of the hidden gems.

LIGHT CODE BATHING

The strongest light codes burst upon Earth at sunrise. This time of day also connects strongly to Lady Aurora – Dawn of the Goddess.

Regardless of whether the sun is shining or not, get up early one morning and go outside at sunrise or just before. If you can see the sun, sit facing it. If not, sit facing the direction of east.

~ Place your hands on your lap, palms facing upwards (receiving), and call in Lady Aurora by saying her name three times.

~ Say, 'Lady Aurora, Lady Aurora, Lady Aurora.'

~ Feel her Divine light begin to infuse you with vibrations of love.

~ Roll up your sleeves or clothing so that your bare skin may be touched directly by the rays; if not visible, imagine them.

~ Keeping your spine straight, take a deep breath in through the nose and out through the mouth.

~ Feel or see the sun's rays washing over you from head to toe.

~ If you have a special ascension request for your personal growth, ask now; for example, you may wish for something like stronger intuition or deeper compassion.

~ Now, in your mind's eye, see these rays penetrating the Solar Plexus chakra a few inches above your belly button.

~ Absorb them for as long as you can, for at least 15 minutes.

~ Give thanks to both Lady Aurora and the sun's portals by taking a bow in gratitude.

This exercise will accustom your body to containing high-vibrational light. You'll be filled with spiritual wisdom and the joys of the sun. Practise it as often as you can, especially when you feel stuck and require an internal shift to take place.

During our spiritual awakening process, we need to remain grounded and keep in mind that we're here to be human. Just go with it if you become indecisive or stuck along the way. Here's an exercise to help you to gain perspective in such times:

CLARITY QUEST

Making a decision can be tricky sometimes. We may fear that we won't get the results that we desire. Other times we may feel unable to proceed because we lack enough information to make an informed choice, so it feels too risky. Lady Aurora says that even the angels have their hands tied at times and if it's for our highest good then answers can be withheld from us.

Have you ever been for a psychic reading and come away with nothing? That's because our angels and guides know that sometimes, knowing the next step of our future could actually hinder it, for we could inadvertently change our destiny by avoiding certain situations. For example, if you were told that you were to meet a new romantic partner who wouldn't last long, but the person you meet afterwards is 'the one', what could potentially happen here? You may conclude that there's no point in entertaining the next person that you meet romantically and wait for 'the one'. But what if you only met 'the one' through this initial brief encounter and by discounting it, you've closed the door on a greater opportunity? The angels know the bigger picture and if we're not ready to see it, then we must trust our gut, our abilities and the knowledge that the angels have our backs at all times. Yet, we can still ask for guidance and clarity in making those decisions, even if we can't perceive the entire outcome.

~ Write down:

   * the dilemma

   * the probable outcomes for each situation

   * the pros and cons

~ Centre and calm your energy now by inviting Lady Aurora into your space.

~ Say, 'Lady Aurora, Lady Aurora, Lady Aurora.'

~ Feel her peaceful energy surround you.

~ Ask her to help you to come to a solid conclusion as to which is the best choice for you to make.

~ Know that this may not be the easiest path, but it's certainly the most rewarding long term.

Look out for signs over the next few days. Lady Aurora will speak to you directly through synchronicities in the external world, such as through the TV, other people's conversations, the radio or in an article in a magazine.

Write Your Destiny

For this next exercise you'll need a pen and a blank sheet of paper:

~ Imagine you've travelled 12 months into the future and you're writing a report of how the previous year turned out, month by month.

~ Remember to make this the year that your deepest wishes came true.

~ Include how excited you felt when you received good news.

~ Be descriptive.

~ Where were you when these exciting events took place?

~ What were you wearing?

~ Were you with anyone?

~ Really connect with the positive emotions of how you felt.

Look at the report each night before you go to sleep to boost your positive expectations and to drive you towards taking action to bring these dreams alive. Lady Aurora will inspire you to make things happen. As we all know, a dream without a plan is just a wish. She'll work her magic, helping you on your way.

Lady Aurora will be a wonderful friend to you once you get to know her. Being so diverse allows her to help you with both earthly and spiritual living. Her wisdom awaits you.

CHAPTER 4

Lady Charity
Generous Love of the Goddess

Archeia Charity is the sweetest angel that you'll ever meet. She oozes femininity and as her name implies, she's extremely generous in every way. Simply praying or speaking to her alone will uplift your heart, making you feel as though you want to be a good Samaritan by performing good deeds yourself. She pays great attention to every word that you speak, making you feel totally heard, valued and accepted.

Together with her Divine counterpart Archangel Chamuel, her roles on Earth are intended to assist us in restoring our sacred hearts. She helps us to love and forgive ourselves, to manifest loving relationships and to express unconditional love into the world.

Lady Charity's Appearance

Lady Charity appears to me as the most petite of the of the Archeiai. Being her usual thoughtful self, she physically manifests at your height. She does this out of humility and she's just as much humbled to be in your presence as you are within hers. She comes to you as an equal. In a delicate yet just voice, she says, 'Creator loves all creatures great and small, coequal.'

In looks, she very much reminds me of Walt Disney's Aurora in the film *Sleeping Beauty*. Her piercing blue eyes stand out in contrast with her rosy-red cheeks. Long, pure white hair frames her dainty face. She looks so beautiful, wearing a pale pink-and-white robe with a Venus rose symbol embellished just under the neck.

Her aura sparkles many shades of pink that seems to infuse the entire room with a cosy glow when she visits.

Lady Charity's Energy

It feels really amazing to be in communication with Lady Charity. She's utterly charming and her presence nurtures you with a motherly love. All angels are facets of the unconditional love of Source, yet Lady Charity embodies love on a much deeper level than all, she's so pure. I think of her as the Goddess's own heart.

By invoking her presence regularly, you'll become more and more like her. Your own qualities and virtues will surface. You'll notice the good in all people and the beauty in all things. Your energy will become very attractive to others, so expect to accumulate new friends and more visitors!

She reminds me of Mary Magdalene in many ways – a true devotee to the Christos Sophia (gnosis/marriage of the soul) and keeper of the sacred flame of unconditional love: Venus.

Lady Charity will help you to access higher levels of consciousness through your Heart chakra. This energy centre can hold much higher-vibrational frequencies than any other energy centre in your body. She holds the 'feminine half' of the Christ Consciousness frequency, whereas the masculine is drawn into the Crown chakra.

When you 'marry', through the energies of your pure heart and awakened mind (the cross), you become the Christed Consciousness.

Along with the other Archeiai, Lady Charity truly brings out the best in you. She can help you with:

- forgiving yourself and others

- healing the past

- manifesting a soul mate

- attracting new friendships

- opening your heart to giving and receiving love

- becoming more generous

- offering unconditional love and self-love

- awakening your angel heart

- healing relationships

- mending broken bonds

- balancing your emotions

- healing the Heart chakra

- softening your persona

- being kind

Lady Charity's Calling Cards

Here's a list of correspondences to this Archeia's energy. You may start to notice them when you begin working with her:

- Her number is 6. You may notice this number repeatedly in various formations. The number 6 carries the vibration of Venus, the planet of love and the Divine feminine.

- Lady Charity's animals are dolphins, which radiate unconditional love, and orcas, which represent everlasting love. You may notice them on your social media timeline or on a TV advert.

- You might feel a little flutter in your heart when she first comes in. If so, remain calm – this is very common! It's simply the petals of your heart awakening in response to her energy.

- You may feel inspired to be generous towards others when she's around you. You may want to give somebody a gift or to help them in some way, while expecting nothing in return. Being charitable is a heavenly virtue – the more you give, the wider your heart opens to the whispers of the angels.

- Her flowers are of course roses. Roses once again link us to the planet Venus – pink for unconditional love, red for romance and white for purity.

Angel of Self-Love

You're probably already well seasoned on the journey and cultivation of a self-love practice. You may have examined your thinking and beliefs many times, knowing that healing requires plenty of inner work. For most people, self-love is low on the priority list, and even if you do have a self-love practice, it can sometimes feel impossible to make that final shift into total acceptance of self.

No matter where you are on your self-love journey, Lady Charity can help you along your way. She can help you to take your self-appreciation to a deeper level than you're currently at. She'll help you to respect, love and even rejoice in who you are.

Lady Charity says that the Earth is suffering an epidemic of people with low self-esteem and lack of self-acceptance. Perhaps you're unhappy with your weight or your looks, or maybe you're convinced that you're less attractive, sexy or lovable than anyone else.

Archeia Charity advises us never to compare ourselves to others. She serves us with the gentle reminder that we human beings tend to be our own worst critic. What we despise when we look into the mirror and the negative self-talk that we uphold about ourselves often goes unnoticed by other people. They simply overlook our flaws, unlike us.

Lady Charity feels great compassion towards self-loathing people, showing them how to release shame and reclaim self-esteem. She promises that we can all learn to love ourselves, just as we learned to judge and put ourselves down.

Archeia Charity says that being hard on ourselves stems from the way our brains were wired as children. Similar to a computer program, these old beliefs are codes, embedded into the subconscious mind. How we were raised, painful memories and being put down or ridiculed by peers all played a part in creating the foundations of insecurity.

Therefore, you're blameless when it comes to having 'issues' or for being a 'negative' person. What you *are* responsible for is how you deal with triggers in future and the disabling of the 'program' when it comes into your awareness.

Additionally, in today's sales-driven society we're constantly subjected to the world's 'ideal look'. We're bombarded with trends, fad diets, Botox, plastic surgery, airbrushed photos and even face-enhancing apps on our phones. All this serves to do is reinforce that we must strive for a 'perfection' that can never be achieved.

Lady Charity says that in the eyes of the angels and Source, we're already perfect in every way, and this is how you should see yourself, too. You're made in the image and likeness of the Creator, making you perfect by default.

Here's a message from Archeia Charity:

> Dear hearts, if only you could feel the love that we angels, Father God and Mother Goddess feel for you, then you would have faith in your heart. You would be mindful that you are a beautiful Divine child of heaven and that you are loved beyond comprehension.
>
> The truth is, there is no hierarchy. There is no you and I but we. You perceive that you are different from one another and from us angels, but you are not. We all originate from the same Source and so shall we all return to the same Source.
>
> Embrace your uniqueness of your time on Earth. We watch and marvel at you in your grandeur and in your light, if only you knew our adoration.
>
> Celebrate and embrace who you are. You need not change a thing, for there is nothing that you can do in thought, word or deed that would prevent us angels and the Creator from loving you so deeply.

Lady Charity will help you to learn to love yourself. Start now by looking in the mirror and pointing out all the beautiful things that you can see about yourself. Tell the body parts that you dislike that you love them.

Angel Encounter

After giving birth to my first daughter Leah when I was just 22 years old, I deeply began to resent the way my post-pregnancy body looked. My tiny waist and smooth baby skin had been replaced with rolls, lumps and bumps, all of which I was really struggling to accept.

Flicking through glossy magazines, my heart would sink at the sight of the images. Size 0 celebrity mums, posing in their tiny bikinis with flawless toned skin, left me feeling depressed. Why were all the signs of motherhood hidden from view?

Being young and naïve at the time, I failed to realize that these images were actually digitally edited and so I developed quite the complex. I was convinced that there was something wrong with me. Above all, I felt ashamed. I looked different from them.

Out of the blue, I developed irritable bowel syndrome (IBS). Always one to practise what I preach, I began to investigate how I'd manifested these symptoms. What had I been thinking about to cause such a reaction in my body?

In my quest for answers I turned to meditation. It was during an out-of-body experience that my spirit guide Helena took my hand and, in an instant, I found that I'd arrived at the angelic Temple of Love.

This pink-and-gold temple is built of pure crystalline light and consists of 12 circular rooms. I'd been here many times before when working with both clients and Archangel Chamuel.

In this instance I arrived directly at the healing chamber. Lady Charity and Archangel Chamuel stood either side of me, their smiling gazes patiently waiting as I familiarized myself with my surroundings. Lady Charity didn't need to explain who she was, I just knew – this is because the veils of perception simply lift when you're in such high-vibrational places.

Infinite rows upon rows of pink-and-gold Angels of the Healing Hearts encircled us, holding a magnificent arc of light. With their palms now facing me, the choirs of angels began to sing. I felt warm swaddled in their loving chants.

A golden swirl of light appeared upon the rose quartz floor in front of me. It danced to the command of the singing, tracing a circular pattern. When complete, a perfect 3D Venus rose symbol had been created, shimmering before my eyes.

Lady Charity whispered into my ear, 'The way of the Rose.' Instinctively, I stepped into the Venus rose labyrinth. Tall golden walls of light towered over me as I proceeded to conquer the maze. I came across dead end upon dead end. Beginning to feel frustrated, I asked myself what I was doing there. I decided that I wanted to go back to my body and proceeded to think of my big toe – a strange but true technique to pull your spirit back into your physical body when travelling other realms – when Lady Charity's voice emerged. 'Claire, this is the maze of your Heart chakra. The dead ends denote your blockages. Would you like to see what they represent? They're the cause of your symptoms.'

I was slightly confused. I hadn't considered my IBS to be a manifestation from matters of the heart, but still I was intrigued and so I replied, 'Yes, please show me.'

Archeia Charity told me to speak to all of the parts of my body in turn and ask them how they felt. I did as she asked. As I got to my belly a wave of sadness overcame me. I came to realize how hard I'd been on myself, even nasty on occasions. I reflected upon the countless times that I'd stood in front of the mirror and said 'You're disgusting' to my stomach.

Every time I'd done this, I'd unknowingly sent an arrow of poison to myself, eventually manifesting as IBS. As my mind rejected my body, my body rejected my food in response. Immediately I saw how silly I'd been and felt a huge sense of remorse towards myself. Of course I loved my belly! Placing my hands on her, I told her how sorry I was and how grateful I was for all of the things that she does for me.

And without any goodbyes, I was back in my house, lying on the couch. I sat up and had a good cry. It felt good to acknowledge and release the build-up of shame I'd harboured. Afterwards I went to the mirror, rolled up my top and said, 'I love you,' to my belly. Each day I made a conscious effort to be kinder towards myself. I affectionately rubbed creams and oils into my skin while holding loving thoughts until I began to believe them. In less than two weeks my IBS symptoms were gone. Self-hatred had caused mayhem within my temple and self-love had restored it to its former glory.

Lady Charity told me that self-love consisted of eating the correct foods, balancing work, rest and play, and admiring, honouring and praising oneself. She added, 'Once you've learned to love yourself then your heart will be wide open to giving and receiving love in all of your relationships.'

Angel of Loving Relationships

Lady Charity is the ultimate love angel! If you've been unlucky in love and are still waiting to meet 'the one', then she's here to help you to manifest a truly loving relationship. Once you've mastered a good level of self-love and care, then you'll be ready to usher in the perfect person with whom to share your life.

Archeia Charity teaches that 'the one' or 'our other half' has paradoxical meanings. On the one hand, feeling that part of you is missing and that another person will complete you is an illusion, because in truth what your soul is really craving is a connection to Source, not another person. Being connected to your Creator unifies your soul by aligning your masculine and feminine energies – the Divine marriage. Only you can bring this to the table. It's an inside job achieved through applying spiritual wisdom.

On the other hand, your soul does have a twin flame. Like the Archeiai you, too, have a Divine complement. In an ideal world, you'd first master an inner harmony within yourself. Then when you're not seeking anybody or anything externally to grant you happiness, meeting 'the one' would be the icing on the cake.

Lady Charity would like to shed some light on the massive confusion around soul mates and twin flames. A soul mate is a person from your soul family with whom you've had previous past-life relationships, not all of which are romantic affairs!

A soul mate can be a child, mum, dad, wife, sister or even a friend. Sharlene, one of my best friends, is my soul mate. We go way back and have incarnated together frequently. This is because our souls have similar missions – we're seeking similar things. Yet, we haven't lived together in a romantic sense.

My husband, John, is my soul mate, too. He was also my romantic partner in my last lifetime, which was in Germany in the 1920s, whereas my mum and dad were my children in that life. So you see, we incarnate together in our soul pods until we've completed our karmic cycles.

A soul mate can manifest as a kindred spirit or a person who causes you great suffering. At the end of the day, they're offering your soul a lesson to experience what it is that you need to evolve further.

Many clients have come to me for readings to discover whether or when they'll meet a romantic partner. Lady Charity points out that all occurs in Divine timing and what's meant for you won't pass you by. Make a space in your heart for the new to enter by letting go of old attachments and only spending time with people who deserve you.

Angel of Unconditional Love

Lady Charity can help you to refine your spirit and develop beautiful qualities that you may yet have to express fully. These qualities are the building blocks of establishing unconditional love.

If the world has taught you to be tough or to 'take it on the chin', Lady Charity will slowly open your heart again so that you can begin to trust that it's safe to love and can learn that there *are* good people in the world.

If you're struggling to forgive somebody who's hurt you, even if they did something despicable, she'll help you to let go of the pain and anger. Feeling resentful and bitter towards someone is like 'drinking poison and expecting the other person to die'! Detaching from the drama brings you freedom.

Lady Charity teaches that unconditional love is just that, unconditional. Placing terms and conditions upon your love comes from a place of fear. Being supported to grow in whichever way you choose is the way of the heart, the way of love. If you find that you try to restrict or control others in any way - often out of fear of losing them - then invoke Lady Charity to bestow you with grace and flexibility. Accepting people or circumstances that you might not like develops many strengths within your spirit.

Lady Charity generously shares her energy by constantly giving thanks and blessings. This is a wonderful practice that you can adopt, too! Simply say 'Thank you' for all that you receive and ask for blessings as many times as you can remember each day. You could bless your food before you eat, or your journey before you travel. You can bless anything and everything. You'll find that your happiness increases along with those blessings! And the Law of Attraction will bring you more luck. Win-win.

The Love Duo

I mentioned earlier that Lady Charity's twin ray is Archangel Chamuel, 'he who sees God'. Like Lady Charity, he sees the good in all beings and helps you to do the same. Together, these Divine beings will support your quest to become a vessel of unconditional love. In return, loving relationships will blossom all around you as you naturally activate the spiritual law 'as within, so without'. Together, these Archangels hold the frequency of the pink ray, the third ray of Divine love. Their etheric temple of crystalline light resides over St Louis, USA.

Archangel Chamuel

Archangel Chamuel is a very serene angel, a true gentle giant. I've found that he usually manifests just over 2 metres (about 7 feet) in height when you're indoors, but I've also seen him outside standing thousands of feet tall. He has shoulder-length golden hair. His dark pink robes hang loosely in his brilliant glistening-pink aura. You can feel his love upon you, pouring out from his eyes, hands and heart. As his name suggests, he sees the Divine in all beings and encourages you to try to do the same. He says that the Divine is always at work, even in difficult situations. Archangel Chamuel opens our eyes to see the bigger picture.

He's also the angel to call upon to help you to find missing items. If you lose something dear to you, then you can ask him to place a ring of angel light around the object. This will protect your belonging and then draw it back to you at the perfect time. However, there's an often overlooked aspect to 'the angel of lost property' that holds a much deeper meaning.

Archangel Chamuel helps you to find what's missing within you. He'll show you how to fill the inner void when you feel empty or incomplete. He'll breathe love, inspiration and new ideas into your aura. When you tune in to them, you come to realize that nothing outside of you can fill in the gaps on a long-term basis. What your soul is craving, that itch that needs scratching, comes from drinking from the well of love that resides within. Archangel Chamuel inspires you to know God/dess more deeply.

Working with Lady Charity

You may feel your heart awakening just by reading about this beautiful being. She's probably watching over you now, ready to shower you with reams of love. To stimulate your Heart chakra when calling in Lady Charity, you could wear a pink item of clothing, burn a pink candle or inhale some rose essential oil. Full altar instructions follow in this chapter. Listed next are crystals that vibrate on her frequency. Wear or hold them during the exercises to deepen your connection:

Lady Charity's Gemstones

The following crystals have the healing vibrations that resonate with the work of Lady Charity:

- rose quartz
- petalite
- diamond
- pink rhodochrosite
- amazonite
- emerald

Holding or wearing these crystals can enhance your receptivity to Lady Charity. They can also enable you to hear more clearly her wisdom of love and compassion. Call her in to heal and advise you with all matters of the heart.

Invocation: Calling in Lady Charity

For this exercise you will need:

~ a white candle

~ a dried herb bundle for burning

~ matches

Before you start, clear your space with your herb bundle, then you're ready to begin:

~ With the matches in your hand ready, state: 'I light this candle in the name of Lady Charity, the angel of love.'

~ Light the candle.

~ Close your eyes and take some deep relaxing breaths in through the nose and out through the mouth, focusing your attention on your Heart chakra.

~ Think of a person who you love to evoke feelings of deep love within you.

~ Feel unconditional love spread from your Heart chakra, penetrating every single cell in your body.

~ Imagine Lady Charity entering the room from a doorway of light within your Heart chakra.

~ Lady Charity kneels lovingly before you, looking you directly in the eye.

~ She places a glistening white rosebud in the centre of your chest.

~ Feel a deep peace wash over you.

~ Ask Lady Charity to open the petals of your Heart chakra so that you may give and receive more love in your life.

~ Watch as she opens the rose petals of your Heart chakra widely into your chest.

~ Breathe in feelings of love.

~ Breathe out feelings of gratitude.

~ Send love to any people or places by holding loving thoughts towards them with your pure open heart, visualizing them happy and peaceful.

~ Spend as much time as you like getting to know Lady Charity's energy.

~ Bathe yourself in her love – the deepest love you've ever experienced.

You can invoke Lady Charity to assist in maintaining harmony in all of your relationships. By practising the previous exercise you raise your frequency to the highest vibration of love. By doing so, you'll begin to exercise more self-loving habits. When you hold yourself in the greatest image of love, you can truly hold love and compassion for the rest of the world.

I have altars all over my house! I made one specially to manifest this book deal and you can create one to manifest anything you want, too. To increase your chances of attracting a romantic partner or to reignite passion in an existing relationship, a love altar is perfect. It serves as a focal point to direct energy towards your intention. It's also the perfect place to speak to Lady Charity about romance and relationships! Here's how:

MAKING A LOVE ALTAR

First of all, you need to figure out where in your home your feng shui romance corner lies:

~ Inside your home, stand with your back to the front door.

~ The furthest right-hand corner of your house – from where you're standing – is the energy centre that affects your romantic relationships.

~ If this corner is full of clutter, then you'll want to tidy that up right away.

~ This area needs to be clean and clear, so that energy can freely circulate around it.

~ You can use anything as an altar; it can be a window ledge, a table, a blanket or a shelf.

~ If using that corner isn't an option – for example, if there's a boiler there or something – then place the altar anywhere you like, with the help of Lady Charity, as the intention alone will be enough.

Preparing your altar

Romance altars are usually dressed with items placed in pairs, signifying manifesting a balanced relationship. You may like to choose a cloth with which to dress it. A simple piece of material or a scarf will do. Get creative and choose which colours or patterns symbolize love to you. Perhaps a cloth with hearts on it works for you. If you're unsure, choose pink for love and red for passion.

Next, you need to collect a few items to adorn your altar with beauty and love. The following is a list of items that would be perfectly suited to manifesting love with Lady Charity. Choose six items.

~ 2 red or pink candles

~ 2 rose quartz crystals

~ 2, 6 or 12 fresh red or pink roses

~ rose petals

~ The Lovers Tarot card

~ a small bowl of honey or, even better, a clam or scallop shell containing the honey to bring an additional blessing from Aphrodite, the goddess of sensuality

~ rose or ylang ylang incense or oil

~ 2 cinnamon sticks

~   a statue or image of a happy couple or a couple sharing a loving embrace; perhaps something like artist Gustav Klimt's painting *The Kiss*

Building your altar

Building an altar is simply the act of placing your sacred altar items in a special area. When you've discovered where your romance corner lies and have purchased your altar items then go ahead and lay them out! It's straightforward. Here are some simple steps to get you started:

~   Clear the energetic space of the area by tidying, dusting and burning herb bundles in the space.

~   Kneel with all of your items in front of you; for example, either on the floor or on a table.

~   With your hands on your heart, call in Lady Charity to help you to set your intentions.

Depending upon your intention of manifesting a new love or reigniting an existing relationship, choose one of the following steps, then continue:

Manifesting a partner

Say, 'Lady Charity, I ask you to open my heart to receive a blessing of love. Please infuse these items with your beautiful Divine light. May the energy of this love then spread far and wide, reaching out to touch the heart of the person who is ready to give and receive unconditional love. Under the Law of Free Will, I bind no person. I allow and trust that whoever is meant for me will be guided to cross my path, and so it is. Thank you, thank you, thank you.'

Or:

Mending a rocky relationship

Say, 'Lady Charity, I ask you for a blessing. Please open the hearts of both myself and [your partner]. May the flame of passion be reignited within our relationship. Give us the strength to find a way to resolve all conflict between us now. May I see all of the qualities within this person, just as I did when we first met. Thank you for reminding me of how great this person is and for prompting me to show my appreciation more often. May I be more honest, patient and compassionate within this relationship. And so it is. Thank you, thank you, thank you.'

Then:

~   Using your intuition, place the items where feels right upon your altar.

~   Each day, or at least every Friday, the day of love, place your hands over the altar and repeat the prayer to Lady Charity.

Altars serve as great reminders of what we hope to manifest. With the blessings of Lady Charity upon your altar, you'll become a magnet to love.

Lady Charity can help you to release pain from your past. Her heart goes out to you if you've experienced abandonment, betrayal or unrequited love. She says that deep down all human beings are looking for a profound and lasting love. She assures you that true love does exist but asks you to contemplate whether you're open to love or if past experiences barricade the door of your heart.

Lady Charity says that if we hold on to resentment and sadness, we can carry our pain into new relationships. This pain can manifest as a feeling that you mistrust the sincerity of people, or perhaps by being needy of others within your relationships. This could even be what prevents a partner from entering your life. Lady Charity can help you to free up your energy and clear your Heart chakra of old emotional wounds and baggage. Once your energy is free from energetic entanglements, you'll create an opening for love to enter. Recapitulation is a powerful energy healing practice that allows you to sever connections to people of the past, particularity those whom you once held in your heart.

This next ritual includes taking back your lost power and returning energy that you may have taken from them unconsciously:

Recapitulation

It's best to perform this exercise during the waning moon phase or when you're menstruating. You'll need one black and one white candle.

~ With your hands in the prayer position, call in Lady Charity by whispering her name three times.

~ Say, 'Lady Charity, Lady Charity, Lady Charity.'

~ Ask her to hold a love-filled space for you while you perform this exercise.

~ Think of a heart-warming moment to begin to awaken your heart centre and to help you to relax.

~ Taking the black candle in your hands, hold it in front of you, level with your Heart chakra.

~ Visualize Lady Charity taking you on a journey inwards to discover what lies in your Heart chakra.

~ Lady Charity opens the door to your heart portal.

~ In your mind, see yourself now walking through the cave of your heart.

~ Whose energy is occupying this space?

~ Is there anyone's energy hanging around that you'd like to be freed from?

~ See that person walking out of your Heart chakra and stopping to sit and face you. This is the person's higher self, which comes to you in peace.

~ They smile at you.

~ See an energetic cord connecting you to the other person.

~ Each time you say the following affirmations, imagine the cord becoming thinner and weaker.

~ Taking a deep breath in, say, 'I take back my power and disconnect my energy.'

~ Breathing out, say, 'I give you back your power; we are now separate entities.'

~ Repeat the breathwork three times or for as long as you feel is required.

~ Imagine Lady Charity taking a rose quartz sword and cutting right through the cord.

~ Placing her hand on your heart chakra, she 'pulls out' the roots of the cord, leaving you totally free.

~ Light the black candle and place it down on the floor or table in front of you.

~ Know that by lighting the flame you begin to banish all old hurts.

~ Now, take the white candle and hold it in front of you, level with your heart.

~ Ask Lady Charity to fill your Heart chakra with peace and the flame of unconditional love.

~ Light the white candle and say, 'My heart is pure, my heart is free, bound to nothing eternally.'

~ Imagine the glow of the white flame melting away hard feelings in the Heart chakra, replacing any lost energy with unconditional love.

~ Destroy the black candle by either allowing it to burn down fully, or by immediately placing it into a bag and crushing it.

~ Remove it from your property by putting it in an outside bin.

~ Blow out the white candle before it burns out and relight it every day for six days for a few minutes, each time repeating 'My heart is pure, my heart is free, bound to nothing eternally.'

Know that you now have the 'space' for love to enter your life.

Now that your heart space is clear, you may wish to take relationships to the next level. Use the following ritual to bring a close friendship, compassion or love to any area of your life:

PLANTING SEEDS OF LOVE

For this exercise you will need:

~ a packet of seeds

~ a plant pot and soil

~ dried herb bundle to burn

~ matches

Choose seeds that most closely represent whichever area of your life it is where you'd like to draw in love. For new or existing friendships, you could choose carnations. To create harmony with your children, select lavender. For self-love, choose sweet peas. And for romantic relationships, the dianthus 'Romance' carnation is a great choice.

Before you begin, waft the smoke of a cleansing herb bundle all over your items to consecrate them:

~ Call in Lady Charity by calling her name three times.

~ With your hands in prayer position, say, 'Lady Charity, Lady Charity, Lady Charity.'

~ Feel her beautiful aura draw close to yours.

~ Place the seeds in your left hand and clasp them tightly over your Heart chakra.

~ Share your intentions with Lady Charity.

~ Explain where in your life you'd like more love.

~ Ask her to help you to manifest it.

~ Imagine Lady Charity taking a glowing rose-pink seed from her own heart and placing it directly into yours.

~ Breathe deeply and watch as the seed slowly spreads pink light throughout your body.

~ Once your body is filled with light, imagine it expanding out into your aura, blessing every single molecule with pure Divine love.

~ Now, see the love filling the room that you're in.

~ Next, see it permeating throughout the house.

~ You may want to visualize this light touching the heart of another person, bringing them a blessing from Lady Charity.

~ Bringing your awareness back to the seeds in your hand, use the power of thought to infuse them with your wish.

~ Visualize your dream fully manifesting before your eyes.

~ Where are you?

~ What can you see?

~ Can you hear or smell anything?

~ Now see the images clearer and brighter in colour.

~ Allow yourself to tap in to the feelings of excitement as you witness this happy, loving scenario.

~ Now that the seeds are programmed with your desire, carefully plant them.

~ Give thanks to Lady Charity.

Each day when you water your seeds, consciously take a moment to imagine your wish come true. As you nurture the seeds, you also nurture your intention.

Rose-Tinted Glasses

Lady Charity concludes this chapter by reminding us of the spiritual truth that you see what you believe. If you view the world through rose-tinted glasses, then you'll find that a glimmer of love lies within all people. If you expect and freely give love, then it's inevitable that the field of potential will mirror you by presenting you with experiences of boundless love.

Work through the exercises in this chapter and learn to love yourself more. You deserve the very best and that includes deep and meaningful love. Lady Charity will be your loving guide.

CHAPTER 5

Lady Christine
Follower of Christ

Archeia Christine holds the frequency of the golden ray of Christ. Her name doesn't mean that she's a follower of Jesus Christ - although they're very close friends - but rather a devotee of the Christ light. When you understand that Christ is a title and not a name, it quickly clears up religious and patriarchal misconceptions that Jesus was the Christ. In truth, He was a human being who attained the Christ Consciousness.

Archeia Christine will prepare you for your own spiritual enlightenment, just like she has done with many great Masters before you. She'll attune your energy field to the highest possible frequency that you can safely handle at this time, so that you, too, can eventually become crowned with the Christos (anointed) Sophia (wisdom) consciousness (receive spiritual enlightenment).

Lady Christine has been designated with the following roles to carry out on Earth: helping human beings to achieve beautiful, positive thoughts, to be fully present in the moment and showing us how to attain spiritual enlightenment by becoming our own guru.

Lady Christine's Appearance

Lady Christine visits me as a huge golden-yellow aura that emanates around her like rays of the sun. She always greets me with a tender smile and her sapphire blue eyes gently fix upon me knowingly. She wears simple white robes and has a blue-and-gold six-pointed star that glows faintly on her forehead. This symbol represents a balance in heaven and Earth energy, and the bridging of masculine and feminine consciousness.

She looks similar to Lady Charity, with very feminine facial features and shoulder-length, sunshine-coloured hair, although she's somewhat taller than Archeia Charity (by several feet). A crown of white and gold roses rests gently upon her head. Sometimes you may be able to smell them.

She's often accompanied by many smaller angels and cherubim. What's strikingly different is her intensely powerful energy! You certainly feel plugged in to the consciousness of your own divinity (higher self) when calling her in.

Lady Christine's Energy

Lady Christine reminds me of a Zen nun. When her aura meets yours, a wave of calm permeates throughout your body, bestowing you with a feeling of contentedness and wellbeing. She's extremely high vibrational, so if you meditate with her you'll feel a gradual build-up in intensity of kundalini energy that resides at the base of the spine and travels through your chakras, similar to when you practise chanting or deep breathing.

It sometimes feels like you're in slow motion when you're with her. This is because she does indeed slow down time. She does this to help you to become more deeply aware of your surroundings, rooting you firmly into the present.

In the Tarot she represents The Hermit. Being an advocate of gathering your own answers, she'll show you how to connect with your higher-self guidance. If you dedicate yourself to spending precious time with your soul, Lady Christine will walk you right up to the inner cave of knowledge. From there, you'll then enter into the silence, alone. She knows that this is the only way to be illuminated with your own soul, enabling you to discover who you really are and the real purpose of your life. The hermit's cave contains the answers to all that you're seeking.

She can help you with:

- receiving guidance from higher dimensions

- being fully present in the moment

- guiding you on your spiritual ascension journey

- attaining enlightenment

- finding inner peace

- perceiving the good in people and situations

- bridging the Christ heart with the Christ mind

- releasing judgement

- becoming the observer

- detaching from your emotions

- opening your Crown chakra

- tuning in to the wisdom of your soul

- transcending the ego

- bending time

Lady Christine's Calling Cards

Lady Christine may give you some of the following signs to get you to notice her when she's around you:

- Any formations of the lucky number 7 are in alignment with Lady Christine. Angel number 777 brings a message from your angels that you're on the right path, living and serving your Divine life purpose. Lady Christine watches over the 7 dimensions of heaven.

- Her animals are doves and white lions, which illustrate her qualities of purity and grace.

- It's common to experience a hot or tingly sensation on the crown of your head when you're working with her.

- You may develop a deeper awareness of time or have intense moments in the now.

- Her flowers are the white lotus, white lilies and white roses, representing purity.

Angel of Beautiful Minds

Lady Christine can help you to cultivate a beautiful mindset. She teaches you how to truly appreciate everything that you have and serves with the gentle reminder to see the proverbial cup as half full when necessary.

She offers wise counsel and support when you require guidance or peace of mind. She's the queen of rationality, making her the go-to angel when your head gets in a spin over an issue or dilemma.

If you're feeling flustered or overwhelmed by deadlines and hefty work schedules, Lady Christine can intervene and facilitate respite.

She can help you to prioritize your workload so that you hit your targets without overdoing it. Lady Christine says that carving a little time out of your day to enjoy a short meditation is time well spent. Precious moments to pause and gather your thoughts are priceless. If you feel as though you need to power through or think that taking a break is a waste of time, then you probably need it the most! She promises you that you'll be more productive in the long run.

All angels have their unique party tricks! Lady Christine's is the ability to bend time. She can literally slow down or even pause time on your behalf if needed. Being a typical Sagittarian, I've found myself – on more than a few occasions – to be running late or worrying about getting somewhere on time.

When on my way to a few important meetings, I've encountered unexpected traffic jams and called upon the help of Lady Christine. Without fail, she reassembles events so that somehow, miraculously, I always make it with a few minutes to spare. So long as you accept responsibility and only do so from time to time, you can occasionally call her in for emergency backup. She can ensure that you reach your destination on schedule.

Archeia Christine is also the angel to call upon when you're feeling mentally stuck or unproductive. Perhaps you have an essay to write or a creative piece of artwork to finish and you've lost your mojo. Well, she'll clear the cobwebs of your mind and plug you into the higher source of creative intelligence.

She's the ultimate angel of concentration, so if you're struggling to focus on the task at hand, need whipping into shape or are forgetful in general, call her in. Ask her to sharpen your thinking. If you have relatives or friends with dementia or Alzheimer's, you can ask Lady Christine for a blessing for them. She'll then hold them in a comforting embrace amid disorientated thoughts and memory loss.

Light a white candle in that person's name and Lady Christine will direct a blessing at them.

If you're an anxious person, or continually have a sense of urgency about you, always pushing for answers, achievements or results, then call in Lady Christine. She can help you to learn to enjoy the moment and to trust the process that you're experiencing. When you believe that life is working for your greatest good, you can relax knowing that all is well.

Angel Encounter

When I was 19 years old, studying to be a holistic therapist, I was taken under the wing of a shaman – 'Carrion' for the purposes of this book. As her apprentice, I learned to work with the spirit world, herbs, power animals and ritual.

I did surprisingly well at what she taught me. It seemed that I had a knack for lightwork. Of course, I had additional support and unlike her, I only ever worked with the angels by my side. They seemed to give me that extra edge.

I was the happiest I'd ever been in my whole life. For the first time I actually felt that I had a purpose. I'd well and truly come into my own and was buoyantly shining my little light into the world. But with my new-found confidence and wisdom came a lot of attention – people are always attracted to your light.

I consider myself to be a very humble and honourable person, and it was totally unintentional when I eventually became more sought-after than my teacher. A succession of unfortunate events took place in her personal life, dulling that magical sparkle that had once twinkled in her eyes.

As she descended into a downward spiral, her own fears stripped her of her power. Setting in like rot, envy smouldered in her heart. Used to being the 'top dog', she found it beneath her to ask me for help during her dark times. Rather than celebrate what a good teacher she'd once been, instead she chose to turn against me in resentment.

Knowing my fears, she hatched a plan to get me off the scene by attempting to pull me off my spiritual path. Her psychic attacks began. They started with little arrows of darkness to fill my mind with self-doubt, to the extreme of manipulating dark entities to scare me away.

Luckily, I could feel when my space had been invaded, so I was able to undo her nasty work before her ill wishes took full effect. But I was growing tired of the battles and the question did cross my mind whether or not I was really meant to be doing this.

My current dilemma left me with two choices: disappear into the background and hope that Carrion would get bored, or remain true to my calling and pursue the path that my soul had led me towards.

To be honest, I was terrified. But after all I'd gone through in my life and conquered so far, it was a no-brainer. I was going to do this anyway! I knew in my heart that I was meant to be on this path. I was born for this!

I held complete trust and faith in Archangel Michael. He assured me that he had my back and during one of his visits, he brought through Archangel Jophiel and Lady Christine to further assist me with my problem with Carrion. Archangel Michael set about protecting the exterior of my home while I worked on the inside, together with Archangel Jophiel and Lady Christine.

First, Archangel Jophiel instructed me to clean my home physically. As I did so, his angels came in and sang, uplifting the negative energy as they moved from room to room. Light green and bright gold light shone right out of them, infusing around all of my belongings; even the sofa had a glowing aura when they were done. Archangel Jophiel reminded me that I still had a music CD that Carrion had given to me, so he advised me to throw it away immediately to prevent her from using it to link into my energy.

When my home felt lovely and light again, Lady Christine took over. She gave me sound advice on how best to respond. She told me that Carrion would no longer be able to take my energy if I simply withdrew from her. That meant not thinking about her at all – easier said than done.

She explained that your energy is your personal currency (current of energy). Thinking spends your currency and being present in the moment gains you interest. That was my solution with Carrion. I had to stop wasting my energy by feeding her with my thoughts. If she didn't exist in my mind, then she ceased to exist at all in my reality. I took the advice of Lady Christine and I've neither seen nor heard from Carrion again. Although Carrion had started off with good intentions, wanting to heal and teach others, sadly the small voice of wisdom was drowned by her ego.

Can you see in this story how power can be dangerous when in the wrong hands? You must always remain humble. Everything that you do must be in alignment with love and integrity. The ego has two extremes: it can make you feel like you're not good enough, or it can turn into arrogance, fuelling you with a sense of grandeur, convincing you that you're worthier than others. Both ends of the spectrum derive from fear. Lady Christine says that being aware of both the voice of the ego and that of wisdom allows you to take your time to choose your response.

Angel of Presence – in the Now

Lady Christine can help you to place your awareness fully in the now. By getting to know her and by following her guidance, you can learn to expand your awareness both of the self and of the world. She'll take you beyond current conceptions of who you think you are, taking you to a place of stillness where the inner observer resides.

She'll instil patience and discipline in you – qualities that'll enable you to witness your thoughts, people's actions or circumstances without forming an opinion. You'll gain the ability simply to watch. Centring yourself in a place of non-judgement then enables you to perceive life in its complete truth, awakening you to a deeper reality, the unity God/dess consciousness, which is free from personality and ego.

When you're in the present moment, all is well. There's nothing to fear. If your thoughts are projecting into the future or trapped in memories of the past then your spirit is fragmented and incomplete. This is because your thoughts contain your life force energy, and if they're not focused on the present moment then they're scattered about in other dimensions and realities.

The ability to be in the moment is difficult to achieve at first, but with discipline it becomes second nature. You'll notice many benefits from this practice, such as more stable moods, becoming less easily triggered emotionally so you can experience inner peace, increased contentment, less worry, improved concentration, the ability to get things done, less procrastination, more happiness, increased energy and a sense of clarity.

Mindful meditation can train your thinking to be rooted in the moment. As can hooking your energy into the light of Lady Christine with the exercises provided later in this chapter.

Angel of the Buddha Christ Mind

Lady Christine reminds us that we're unlimited, both in terms of what we're capable of and within our evolution. She says that even in our spirituality there's no ceiling to cap the heights to which we may soar. There's a common misconception that when we attain our Christ or Buddha mind, we return to heaven, job done. But this is a half-truth, because while we do rejoin the great pool of Source energy, our ascension journey simply continues. In fact, our evolution is the same as our existence: eternal.

There are dimensions within dimensions that span out for eternity, so although attaining the wisdom of Christ will grant us access into higher dimensions and realties, there's no actual finish line. That may seem pretty deep, but there really is no need to feel overwhelmed! All that's required of us is to take one step at a time.

Lady Christine is the perfect angel to ensure that we stay focused on our current mission, in which all human beings are partaking. Whether you walk the spiritual path in this lifetime or in 10 lives from now, regardless, we're all headed for the same destination: the fifth dimension and beyond.

Lady Christine explained to me that the chakra system can be looked upon as a map to navigate through your journey to enlightenment. As we know, spiritual time is nonlinear, so the order that you work through the chakras is flexible, yet it's good to start at the beginning, at the Root chakra. This involves us facing our fears, becoming confident, standing on our own two feet and so forth.

This will create a solid foundation on which your spiritual house is built. Lady Christine advises us to power through rather than give in to the temptation of skipping working on the 'boring' chakras. Sure, it's much more fun to experiment with, say, the Third Eye chakra rather than the Solar Plexus or the Throat, but you'll discover just as many treasures for your soul's growth with each and every one.

She assures us that this is a natural urge because the lower chakras force us to embrace our shadow and shed old skins and traumas, which is unpleasant, unlike having a psychic vision, which is very empowering and exciting. The problem is, when we've had lots of activity within our Third Eye chakra and have neglected the lower energy centres, we can encounter a very common trick of the ego: the Battle of the Two Snakes. Just like my teacher, Carrion, did.

Lady Christine works with all people who are ready to step up to the next level of their spirituality. She'll connect your Crown chakra directly to the stream of light of the Divine mind of God/dess. Lady Christine will shape you into becoming your own guru, meaning you won't require teachers or guidance from anyone else once you reach this phase of your growth. All of the answers that you could ever need will be accessible from within you. She says:

We angels are overjoyed that you are seeking us out and coming to understand and reclaim your divinity. Your entire spiritual heritage is yours for the taking. It is a hidden treasure, concealed deep within you. You may have travelled the entire world, read hundreds of books and attended many seminars, but what you were looking for was elsewhere, because the pearl of wisdom was within you all along.

And so, I invite you to call upon me during your meditations. I will expand your consciousness and instruct you on the bridging of your masculine and feminine energies, until your heart and mind sing the same song. This is where you will then be capable of initiating yourself into the mysteries of the soul, of the cosmos, so you can become one with the Creator.

The Golden Duo

Lady Christine's twin ray is Archangel Jophiel, whose name means 'Beauty of God'. These serene angels hold the frequency of the golden ray of Christ and are keepers of the flame of wisdom. They work together by opening up and attuning our Crown chakra to receiving the Divine teachings of Christ.

Their etheric portal is located near Lanzhou, China. You can link in to the energies of this place by simply singing Archangel Jophiel's (Jo-fee-ell) or Lady Christine's (Chris-teen) name.

Archangel Jophiel

Archangel Jophiel is very sweet. There have been many debates among angel enthusiasts on whether he is in fact male or female. This is partly down to how artists have made him look so beautiful. They'll have portrayed him in this feminine way because this is how they'd have felt being around him, as he's very gentle and even somewhat motherly.

He appears to me with soft golden-brown shoulder-length hair and dark brown eyes. Like Lady Christine, he wears a white bell-sleeved robe, only his has a large golden cross over his chest. There are often little blue birds and white doves that come through with him. He's rather like Snow White, clearing up the energies of your home but with his little winged helpers.

Archangel Jophiel has a very deliberate disposition. He performs tasks slowly and very intently – think snail's pace! He's very delicate in movement, unlike some of the other angels – Lady Ariel or Archangel Michael for example – who'll whoosh into your space.

Archangel Jophiel can help you with all of the same tasks as Lady Christine, but from a masculine perspective. Lady Christine can open you up to receiving wisdom and Archangel Jophiel can help you to become that wisdom by providing circumstances or lessons so that you can truly embody Christ through action.

He reminds us that it's easier to have a positive mindset if we spend regular time in nature, taking time to enjoy beautiful places such as waterfalls and woodlands. Archangel Jophiel is the king of feng shui! He can help you to transform your living space totally, whether that be a simple lick of paint or a full-blown detox of your home's energetic blueprint. Call upon Archangel Jophiel to help you to plan and create a peaceful sanctuary at home.

Simple tips from Archangel Jophiel to get you on your way include:

- reducing clutter

- giving away anything that you dislike

- surrounding yourself with colours, items and pictures that you love

You can also call upon him if you feel as though you need an energetic spring-clean. If you've had a dispute with a neighbour or had a fall out at home and the energy feels tense, ask him to lighten the space.

Working with Lady Christine

Lady Christine is a beautifully uplifting angel with whom to work. She can help you to connect to your higher mind and the supreme Divine intelligence. As we step up our evolution she'll help us to keep our feet firmly on the ground to ensure that we don't get too carried away with our newly born spiritual powers, and that we remain loving and wise. Before you set out to work with this beautiful angel, it would be a good idea to read through the following exercises. Be sure to clear your space before you practise. For her altar, I use everything in white and burn frankincense essential oil.

Lady Christine's Gemstones

The following crystals have healing vibrations that resonate with the work of Lady Christine:

- azurite
- golden healer quartz
- aquamarine
- selenite
- healer's gold
- rose quartz
- spirit quartz

These gemstones can further assist in you making a strong connection with Lady Christine's energy. They'll enhance your ability to receive her wisdom directly and will support any healing intentions that you may want to work on with her help. Try this invocation and experience Lady Christine's energy for yourself:

 INVOCATION: CALLING IN LADY CHRISTINE

For this exercise you will need:

~ a white candle

~ matches

~ a pen and a piece of paper

To call in Lady Christine:

~ Light a white candle and with your hands in prayer posture, recite the following invocation three times: 'Lady of Wisdom, Lady of Light, Lady Christine's flame I ignite. Christed in mind, Christed in soul, the Christos Sophia I now uphold.'

~ Focus your attention on your Crown chakra, your 1,000-petalled lotus.

~ Imagine the petals beginning to stretch wide open.

~ From above, Lady Christine pulls a golden thread of light upwards from the centre of your crown.

~ See the shimmering thread travelling higher and higher until it reaches the blue star Sirius.

~ Allow your thread to latch on to Sirius and begin drawing down ascension Christ codes through your thread in rays of gold and blue.

~ Allow yourself time to dream – be visually creative.

~ When you're ready, draw down your golden thread and close the petals back over the Crown chakra.

~ Record your experience on paper.

~ Tap your body all over and stamp your feet for as long as you need to ground your spirit back into the Earth.

~ Give a big thank you to Lady Christine.

This exercise will open your Crown chakra to receiving the wisdom of the golden ray of Christ, the gateway of the Masters. Drawing in light codes under the supervision of Lady Christine will speed up your ascension process and help you to enjoy the journey all the more. Working in alignment with Lady Christine can prevent you from dipping into ego when you feel the power of the Divine coursing through you. This is what I explain next.

The Duel of the Two Snakes

Earlier in this chapter, I briefly mentioned an ego trick called the Battle of the Two Snakes. All the highly evolved spiritual people I know have endured this test, often more than once. As we journey through our chakra awakening, we inevitably reach elevated states of consciousness. It's when we're on the cusp of enlightenment that the two snakes within us, Ida and Pingala, will meet at the Third Eye gate, ready to duel. The masculine and feminine within you will either unite as one, or slip into the shadow reality if they succumb to the final trick of the ego. The trick is that when our ego becomes inflated by our new-found wisdom, we believe ourselves to be special or better than others.

Passing the duel (transcending duality consciousness) grants you access to the gate of Christ consciousness, the Crown chakra. Passing through the Third Eye gate is achievable only by being humble and not being duped at the last hurdle. You may find it difficult to believe that this would happen to you or anyone who has good intentions, but you'd be surprised!

Unfortunately, this is all too common and I've personally witnessed countless people get caught out by the Third Eye gate. Which is why Lady Christine insisted that I covered it in this chapter. If I had a pound for every person who thinks that they're the incarnation of Mary Magdalene, Isis or Jesus, I'd be a very wealthy woman!

This is how the ego snare works: a rapid spiritual awakening is occurring in many individuals. This double-dimensional leap means that a huge amount of knowledge is available like never before, yet there's a difference between knowledge and wisdom.

As channels become so easy to open, direct access to the angels, Ascended Masters and all celestial beings is granted. From this position, you come into huge amounts of spiritual power. Everything is achievable and you quite literally become superhuman. The problem then arises, because it's so easy to confuse the memories of the Masters as your own. Coming from a long period of having a separate identity, it's inconceivable to have a joint memory bank in the planes of the Akasha (non-physical). Logically, how would you know such intimate, detailed information?

What further enhances confusion is when other people recognize the power in you and also assume that you're an incarnated heavenly being.

I once did a Skype reading for a lady in Italy. At the end of the reading she asked me, 'Are you Mary Magdalene?' I replied, 'No, I'm nobody special.' In truth, I know that I am special, we all are, but no more than anyone else. I refuse to let it go to my head. The client was accurate in picking up on the energies of Mary Magdalene. I'm her priestess, so of course my client will feel her around me. I call upon her energy to work through me, to help me to be true and to be my best. Lady Christine says that gratitude and humility will help you to keep your feet firmly on the ground.

Acknowledging the Inner Shadow

With the guidance of Lady Christine, this is a very powerful kundalini awakening exercise that you can use to ensure that you're healing your consciousness as well as upgrading it. This will reveal to you any shadow aspects that need clearing at each of the chakra gates. Failing to look at the shadow becomes very apparent when your consciousness rises to that of the Crown chakra. If the necessary inner work has been overlooked, then just as in the mythical story of The Tower Tarot card, the structure of the building will collapse once struck by the lightning of Source (the subconscious becoming conscious), causing all kinds of unexpected mayhem.

Working through the shadow means you'll be unshakable when you reach your peak.

SHEDDING LIGHT ON YOUR SHADOW

This is a very long exercise, so ensure that you have enough time to go through it undisturbed.

You will need:

~   A pen and a sheet of white paper handy to take notes afterwards

I recommend burning frankincense resin or essential oil during this exercise to cleanse the space around you as you delve into your shadow aspects:

~   Close your eyes and take several deep breaths in through the nose and out through the mouth.

~   Call in Lady Christine by whispering or singing her name three times.

~   With your hands in the prayer position, say, 'Lady Christine, Lady Christine, Lady Christine.'

~   From the centre of your Heart chakra, send out your light both upwards towards the sky and downwards towards the Earth simultaneously.

~   See this light as a solid column of light travelling through your core, awakening each chakra as it passes through them.

~   The column of light below passes through your Earth Star chakra and reaches all the way down to the centre of the Earth.

~   Visualize it connecting magnetically to the light of the Divine Mother.

~   Draw up feminine Earth energy through your column and allow it to sit in the Root chakra.

~   Next, focus on the end of the column of light that stretches out through the top of your head.

~   Visualize it travelling up through the sky and into space.

~   It comes to a stop and joins Sirius, the blue star of the Divine masculine.

~   In a spiral motion, draw down light from Sirius through the top of your column, passing each of the chakras until you reach the Root chakra.

~   Allow the energy to rest here and mingle with the light of Earth.

~   See and feel your Root chakra brimming with powerful, healing ascension light.

~   Bring your awareness to the space directly below the Root chakra.

~   Now, see two snakes emerging from this space.

~   The snake on the left-hand side is black and the one on the right is gold.

~   Watch as the snakes weave their silky bodies, crossing through your Root chakra, consuming the mixture of light.

~   They spread the light through each of the chakras as they make their ascent to your brow.

~   Taking your time, see or feel each chakra being infused with the mixture of light from both above and below.

~   The snakes come to a standstill at your Third Eye chakra, staring at each other directly in the eye.

~   Take a deep breath in.

~   Now, imagine Lady Christine handing you a black obsidian scrying mirror.

~   By viewing yourself through the mirror you gain access to a view of lifetimes of suppressed pain, trauma, ancestral karma, inherited negative beliefs, selfish traits and all of the darkness that you'd rather not see, wishing it to remain hidden in the shadows.

~   Hold the mirror over your Root chakra.

~   Does fear or shame reside here?

~ If so, name it and offer it to Lady Christine.

~ Watch as she immediately transforms existing energy with her golden energy and purifies your space, making it lighter and brighter.

~ Taking the mirror up to the Sacral chakra, what's revealed here?

~ Sexual shame?

~ Regrets?

~ Loss?

~ Name them and hand them over to Lady Christine for transmutation.

~ Moving on to the Solar Plexus chakra, what does the mirror reveal?

~ Ego?

~ Greed?

~ Hunger for power?

~ If so, state them and hand them to Lady Christine for healing.

~ Travelling to your precious Heart chakra, what's reflected from your shadow?

~ Pride?

~ Selfishness?

~ Infidelity?

~ Lack of trust?

~ Clear your Heart chakra by bringing it to Lady Christine's light.

~ Moving on to the Throat chakra, what does the black mirror reveal?

~ Words of regret?

~ Words that went unspoken?

~ A lack of trust in oneself?

~ Name what resides in your shadow and hand it to Lady Christine for purification.

~ Finally, you reach the Third Eye chakra, where your snakes patiently await.

~ Holding the mirror over the Third Eye chakra, you see a reflection of your shadow self aspect.

~ What does your inner shadow reveal to you about your ascension journey?

~ Does she feel that you require further work on any of the lower chakras?

~ If so, ask what it is that you must do.

~ Smile at your shadow self and give her a hug.

~ With a sense of respect and honour, tell her it's time to step into the light.

~ Lady Christine showers both you and your shadow self in the golden rays of Christ light.

~ Illuminating all darkness, she transforms and uplifts your energy.

~ A golden doorway begins to open within the Third Eye chakra.

~ The snakes grant you access to the gate of the Crown chakra.

~ Give thanks to Lady Christine and to the light of Sirius and the Earth.

~ Visualize your column of light drawing back into your body, disconnecting you from the energy sources that you'd tapped in to.

~ Close down each chakra by seeing them in your mind's eye as a flower closing its petals over.

~ Take a deep breath in through your nose and out through your mouth.

~ Rub your hands together.

~ Feel the physicality of your body.

~ Slowly bring yourself back to the here and now.

~ Take notes of the guidance you received on your journey.

Most people have negative feelings and fears lurking in the shadow aspect of their personality. It's part of the human journey to experience such emotions, so be proud of yourself for taking the time to review your own fears. Failing to address the shadow results in repeating the same life lessons. The way to personal freedom is embracing, healing and accepting the shadow. Alchemize your fears into wisdom.

Similarly, after the Battle of the Two Snakes exercise it's likely that you'll be tested in the physical world to see if you really have transcended the trips of the ego. Any triggers or challenges that arise over the coming weeks or months will speed up your spiritual progress. Be mindful of them and remember, Lady Christine will ensure that you're only given what you can handle.

⌒

Lady Christine was one of many light emissaries who guided Yeshua (Jesus) and Mary Magdalene on their ascension journey. It was after Yeshua's passing that the Archeiai appeared to go underground for the next 2,000 years. With the domination and brutality of the Roman Catholic Church, it took only two generations and they were completely forgotten.

This is one of the initiations that Lady Christine gave to Mary Magdalene in the Pyramids of Egypt. After she lost her beloved Yeshua, Mary became the sole carrier of the Christ flame on Earth. The flame continues to burn through the lineage of women who came after her: the Sisterhood of the Rose, witches and mystics. Every minute, the Magdalene Christ flame grows stronger. Have Mary Magdalene and the mysteries of women been calling you? Try this next exercise to bring you closer to discovering your Holy Grail:

ACTIVATING THE CHRIST FLAME

Reactivating the Christ flame within you will help to heal both yourself and the disenfranchisement of women. This exercise will awaken your sleeping feminine wisdom – the aspect of Christ that we haven't yet been taught about:

You will need:

~ a pen and a sheet of white paper

~ a white candle

~ matches

~ rose essential oil and a burner

~ an offering of a fresh rose for Mary Magdalene and all of the generations of women both before and after who kept our sacred heritage alive

When you're ready, let's begin:

~ Light your oil burner, adding 4 drops of rose oil to the water.

~ Light the candle and dedicate it by saying: 'I dedicate my light to the Magdalene flame, my feminine heritage I now reclaim, Christine, Sophia, Isis, Mary.'

~ With your eyes now closed, try to see or sense these Divine feminine wisdom keepers surrounding you, protecting and loving you.

~ Open your Heart chakra by visualizing a huge white rose opening in the centre of your chest.

~ Breathe deeply, in through the nose and out through the mouth.

~ Lady Christine steps forwards and sits closely on your left-hand side.

~ Feel her eternal stillness washing over you, bringing you even deeper feelings of peace.

~ Next, Mary Magdalene step forwards and sits closely by your right-hand side.

~ Feel her compassion and unconditional love washing over you.

~ You're now filled with the deepest feelings of love.

~ Mary Magdalene places her gentle hands over your Heart chakra and Lady Christine places hers upon your Crown chakra.

~ You feel both of these areas beginning to tingle and grow warm.

~ Focusing on your Heart chakra, breathe in and visualize your heart energy travelling up in a channel towards your Crown chakra.

~ As you exhale, watch the energy travel back down the channel from the Crown chakra to the Heart chakra.

~ Repeat this three times.

~ After three cycles state: 'Christ in heart, Christ in mind, old tales, old skins left behind. Make me fresh, build me anew, a rising feminine leader, I am true. Heart and mind join as one, God and Goddess bless what I am to become.'

~ At the same time, Mary Magdalene lights a pink flame in your Heart chakra while Lady Christine lights a gold one in your Crown chakra.

~ You've now activated the Christ flame.

~ Spend as much time as you like in this high state of awareness.

~ Mary Magdalene and Lady Christine may have a direct message for you – trust whatever comes to mind.

~ Your guides step back. You thank both them and all of the loving souls who are present.

~ Take a quick deep breath in and as you exhale, chant, 'Yaaammm.'

~ The rose in the centre of your heart retracts into a bud as you chant this sacred sound.

~ Open your eyes.

~ Take the silky rose into your hands and inhale the rich scent.

~ Fully ground your energy by moving your body.

~ Take notes of any additional visions or messages that you received.

~ Leave your rose in a special place, offering it up with gratitude.

Well done! You've mastered reigniting your own Christ flame! Rest assured, the angels and Masters will be rejoicing that you're evolving your own self-mastery skills. This exercise will help you to obtain the missing piece of the ascension puzzle, the Christ that was withheld from us. I'm truly excited for you and what you're going to unearth by using these practices.

Remember, the world needs your light. Every time you perform this and the other exercises, you bring more Christ light to the entire planet. Lady Christine will remind you to be proud of yourself while remaining graceful and humble.

CHAPTER 6

Lady Faith
Trust in the Goddess

Archeia Faith is a swift and solid warrior-ess angel – only what you'd expect being the twin flame of the one and only Archangel Michael. Her name, 'Faith', reminds us that there's always a bigger hand at play. Although we don't see the grander picture in its entirety from our limited physical form, we must trust in it all the same. Lady Faith will help you to develop that trust, not only in God/dess and the Divine plan, but also within yourself and your own capabilities.

As well as instilling trust and faith in you, her other major task is in leading the Army of Light. The Legions of Light protect the masses on a grand scale, ensuring that universal spiritual laws are upheld. On a smaller scale, she overlights shamans, healers and anybody else who's frequently subjected to dense energy for the good of others. If you're a healer of sorts, she'll help you to become spiritually strong and self-reliant. With her knowledge you can learn how to mature your energy body. In other words, become a walking shield wall.

Lady Faith's Appearance

Just like Archeia Ariel, Lady Faith also has two physical looks depending on the situation in which you encounter her. During casual visits when she comes to guide and teach you, she's usually dressed rather elegantly. For me, she somewhat resembles a school principal with her neat blonde hair and her regal attire, consisting of a long white silk dress and a dark blue cloak.

Yet, upon the onset of potential threat or danger, she can look very different. Armed with shield and sword, she'll whoosh in like a Norse shield-maiden ready for action. When she appears like this you know she means business. It's her way of saying 'put your guard up'. Her huge cobalt-blue aura fills the entire room, sucking up lower energies and churning them back out transformed into vibrant, crystal-clear ki.

Faith's Energy

Just as she has two different looks, Lady Faith also has two different feels. Regardless of her demeanour, you'll still be able to recognize her underlying dynamic energy. She does have a seriousness to her personality, which is the total opposite of Archangel Michael's. As you probably already know, he's a real hoot.

This Archeia doesn't mess around and encourages you to adopt an attitude of 'getting things done'. Although she gets straight to the point, she's still deeply loving and compassionate. When you're down, she'll nurture you and help you to heal by reminding you of your truth: you're a warrior of light in the making. She'll help you to move on mentally by revealing necessary truths in a gentle way, and by helping you to shed restrictive energetic cords to people and places.

If you become her apprentice, she'll toughen you up, empowering you to fight your own battles. Equally, she'll also step in and fight your corner if you're out of your depth. She's always there for you when needed. In the Tarot deck she represents Lady Justice. She brings truths to light, fights for equality, protects the innocent and restores faith in humanity. She's the archetypal shield-maiden, warrior-ess of light, slayer of darkness and illuminator of truth.

She can help you with:

- speaking your truth
- trusting in the Divine
- trusting yourself
- trusting others
- healing betrayal between women
- strengthening your aura
- healing the Throat chakra
- protecting your space
- removing negative energy
- being fair and just
- being honest
- achieving psychic protection
- developing confidence
- believing in yourself

Lady Faith's Calling Cards

If you're not frequently meditating or you take long breaks from your spiritual practice then your extrasensory perception (ESP) can become numb, unless you were born with your psychic gifts awakened, in which case your awareness can easily zone out. Luckily, the angels want you to seize every opportunity, so they'll send subtle signs to remind you that they're available to assist, just as soon as you give the go-ahead.

Here are Lady Faith's bespoke signature calling cards to help you recognize her energy:

- Her number is 444. Regarded as 'the' angel number, 4s represent balance and protection from the 4 corners, or it can be doubled up to the 8 directions.

- Her spirit animal is the eagle, a fearless, majestic hunting bird that rises high into the sky, obtaining a much bigger picture.

- When she comes in, your Throat chakra may start to expand, feeling as though it's swelling. This is a classic symptom of the spirit wanting to express itself. Take a pen and paper if this happens and write down anything that comes to you from your higher self-guidance.

- You may feel protective towards others when you've been working with her. You'll feel empowered to face head on anything out of alignment or that lacks integrity.

- Her flowers are daffodils, which will help you with speaking your golden truth.

Angel of Truth

Have you asked yourself 'who am I?' or 'why am I here?' If so, then you're a seeker of truth. Lady Faith is the angel of truth and will act as your light bearer, guiding you on your discovery of self. She can show you where your soul originated, which will then give you instant access to hidden gems of wisdom that were locked into the DNA of your soul. She can help you to identify answers to the most common questions that I hear lightworkers ask, such as who you are, where you've been and, most importantly, what you're here to accomplish.

Not only does she reveal to you the meaning of your spiritual truths, but she also teaches you to become an authentic and true person. She helps you to become really genuine in all of your actions and astutely accurate in your observations. She does this by allowing you to see beyond the surface of situations in order to reach the true meaning that lies beyond your personal judgements.

She's now reminding me of the quote by Jesus: 'The truth shall set you free.' She says, 'When you understand who you are, you are no longer bound to the ego mind or limitation.'

If you have an issue or fear that you need to rectify, even from a past life, Lady Faith will help you to purge all negativity that distorts your highest truth, including debris locked within the timelines of your soul. She'll show you your forgotten stories and memories that require slaying and purifying from your psyche. This process can be such a relief, as I've experienced myself; I'll explain this in my next story.

Angel Encounter

The first time that I met Lady Faith eludes me. She's another one of the angels whom I've always known. It would be like asking me when was the first time I saw my cousin, grandad or auntie. She's just always been there. But I'd like to share a tale of one of my experiences so that you can get a feel of how you can work with her, too.

When I was younger, I had an irrational fear of being in confined spaces, such as lifts or public toilet cubicles. I suspected that this fear could be linked to a past-life experience, so during a meditation one day I asked Lady Faith to show me whether or not my hunch held any validity. Regardless, I wanted to know at what point in my life (or lives) I'd developed this pesky hindrance. What was triggering this irrational fear?

After about 20 minutes of controlling my breath with pranayama practice, my astral body was ready and off we travelled through the dimensions. Sure enough, Lady Faith took me back to a previous incarnation where I worked as a text scribe in ancient Egypt. Specializing in funerals, my job entailed painting magical inscriptions and spells onto the tomb walls, coffins and sarcophagi. But when our young pharaoh died unexpectedly, there was much to prepare and inevitable shortcuts were taken. The royal funeral was rushed to say the least.

Now, as with most great historical stories, a scandal followed this death. Jealous of the late king, his successor wanted to erase all evidence that he'd ever existed. With this in mind, he ordered both myself and another artist to ensure that the inscriptions on the coffin were incomplete. He also demanded that we covertly deface the map of instructions that were beautifully laid out on the tomb walls. In the successor's eyes, surely this violation would be enough to ensure that the late king would be unsuccessful in navigating his way through the underworld, as without the correct instructions to follow, he'd definitely fail to secure resurrection in the afterlife.

Failing to obey the cruel requests of the successor, his guards threw both of us workers into the tomb, just as it was about to be sealed for the last time. We died crying in each other's arms, sealed up in that tomb, starving and afraid in the darkness.

It was such a revelation to remember this had occurred to me. My fear of being in lifts and small spaces began to make sense as I recalled the feelings of claustrophobia and intense fear from all that time ago. Remembering this truth alone was enough to free me from my irrational fear. Afterwards, if I ever felt slightly anxious, I knew the reason why and calm was immediately restored. Another layer of cladding was shed, pushing me closer to the core of who I truly am, thanks to our Lady of Faith.

The icing on the cake came a few years later, when one of my best friends said, 'Do you remember when we died in Egypt in that tomb?' I've got goose bumps just writing it, as I'd never shared the story with anyone until now.

Angel of Faith

'Blessed are those who have not seen yet have believed.'
John 20:29

Lady Faith can help you to maintain your faith in an unjust world. She's that knowing within you that trusts that the universal scales of balance will inevitably realign, enforced by the Law of Karma. She reminds us that it's not our job to judge or condemn others. And because nobody escapes the spiritual law of cause and effect (every action has a reaction), you need not be concerned with the acts of others. She helps you to trust that everything is being handled accordingly. If other people's actions concern you, then hand it to Lady Faith and she'll shield you from the harsh or cruel actions of others.

If you've been struggling with challenges and life is looking bleak, Lady Faith can help you to hang on in there. She promises that every cloud has a silver lining. Furthermore, she'll help you to truly believe that everything happens for a reason, always trusting that the universe is on your side.

Faith is one of the magical ingredients required to cook up successful manifestations. If you're struggling to manifest your dreams, ask yourself: Do you really believe that you can have it? If not, call upon this Archeia and ask her to fill you with the faith that your prayers will be answered. Like they say, faith can move mountains.

Lady Faith also adds that:

> Living in a state of trust and having faith in yourself is paramount to your spiritual ascension. As your superhuman powers evolve, you must trust in them in order to utilize them to your fullest potential. How else could you reclaim your God/dess self if you constantly rely upon the good opinion of others? You have everything inside of you already. Tap in to your wisdom and unleash your gifts. By having faith in yourself, everything is achievable.

Lady Faith believes in you 110 per cent. How do you think your life would look if you held just half that amount of confidence in yourself? I tell you, it would look amazing, because I know – I've been there myself. By building a sense of faith in myself, I successfully created the life that I wish to live. I have a wonderful family and my job is my joy. And that's enough for me – I'm very happy and satisfied.

Even if you've had the worst luck ever, and even if all of your life you've only ever known suffering, Lady Faith will gradually help you to build your faith. She can help you to become a lot more optimistic, and just see what happens when you do – faith grows!

Angel of Trust

Lady Faith can help you to develop a sense of trust in others. We've all had our fingers burned in the past and that can leave us doubtful whether or not we can trust people. But we can't allow past experiences to taint our expectations or to project upon others.

Lady Faith is very passionate about bridging broken bonds and restoring trust between men and women, but especially among the women at this time. The Age of Aquarius heralds the return of sisterhood and it'll be the harmony between women that restores our communities. This grand rebuild has already begun, but we must continue to establish a sense of trust between ourselves.

Over the years I've witnessed many spiritual teachers become very territorial about their clients and their workshops. Lady Faith says that being raised within a masculine mindset society can give us the urge to be slightly dominant. It's almost instinctive to 'protect' what we've created. However, it serves to remind us that we don't truly own anything.

She explained to me that although we're the ones who birth ideas into physical life, in reality every single idea comes from the great universal mind of Father God, Mother Goddess. She adds that if we cling to our projects in fear of being copied or excelled then we've become enslaved to an illusion that will then contaminate our life with fear.

If you find yourself naturally becoming overprotective and afraid to share, remember to call upon Lady Faith for support. There's no shame in admitting that your shadow has been triggered. In fact, it's quite the opposite. The angels smile when we acknowledge our fears, as it's a sign of spiritual maturity.

Lady Faith is helping women to come to terms with the massive betrayal among us, otherwise known as the witch wound. It's likely that many of you reading this book were affected by the horrific witch trials. Whether you were there or not, the wounding lives on through our ancestral lines. We've inherited it. Our wombs are still haunted with guilt and shame of the forced betrayal that was endured. If you feel this deeply and it resonates, call in Lady Faith to restore the trust among the women in your life. Ask her to heal your pain. And remember to extend your prayers to our fellow sisters and brothers, too.

There are many wrongs to be righted in our unbalanced world, but trust in this process, too. After this massive period of injustice and suffering, the wheel must turn and all of the goodness that we are owed, all of the joys, the love and harmony is karmically ours to reclaim now.

Angel of Self-Defence

As I stated earlier, the Piscean Age of the Guru is no longer valid. The fifth dimension and beyond demands that you're strong enough to protect your own energy without relying on anyone, even the angels.

Archangel Michael is renowned as the angel of protection. He's the SOS angel to call upon in any fearful situation. But Lady Faith asks you to take things up a notch. She teaches you how to develop your own psychic shields and empowers you with the courage to stand on your own two feet during energy battles.

You can relax knowing that she'll stay by your side while you develop and strengthen your aura. Her aim is to stand back and stand guard, allowing you to evolve, eventually becoming powerful and brave without having to call upon external forces to shield you. She'll mould you into a peaceful warrior, able to fight your own battles, to slay your own demons and to own your own shadow, whatever that may be.

It's fine to call upon the Angelic Kingdom for protection. In fact, it's strongly advised that you do so, for the first few years at least. But it's worth noting that at some point relying on anything outside of you keeps you limited. Lady Faith knows that you have unlimited potential. The more you push your comfort zones, the more you'll expand into new territories. And with each rub against the grain, you carve out a greater version of yourself.

Lady Faith says that when you feel ready, call upon your own spirit for protection and remember to ask her to mentor you. So long as you've made a lady's agreement with Lady Faith, if you get in above your head she'll step in and intervene – she's got your back. So, effectively, working with Lady Faith is more like a practice run than being thrown in at the deep end.

I frequently used to call upon Archangel Michael for protection. I'll always remember the first time he just stood there while I dealt with a psychic battle by myself. He was the one who told me that I had to toughen myself up and to work with Lady Faith. I was so dismayed I went straight to a fellow angel expert for their opinion. We cried, laughing when we realized that the same thing had happened to both of us. The angels are expecting more from us!

In order for your shields to be strong you need to have a pure mind, a strong body and an even stronger spirit. Lady Faith says:

Beloved ones, your faith will be tested many times upon your ascension path. Circumstances arise that challenge you mentally, weaken your body and batter your spirit, so how do you maintain your strength during these times? Call upon me, that is how. I will imbue you with courage. I have faith in you. I believe in you, your dreams and your potential. When faith is low, ask and I will light the flame of truth brightly within you. You will become the light that guides you.

The Sword Duo

Archangel Michael is the masculine twin flame counterpart to Lady Faith. Together, they uphold the light of the blue ray – the first spectrum of light that emerged from our Creator. The blue ray angels use their cobalt-blue light to ensure that the four corners of the planet are protected. Archangel Michael will lend you his cloak and shield to protect you from external negative influences. He's only too happy to do this for you, but at some stage of your spiritual training you'll be required to learn to do this for yourself.

At first, it can be very daunting if you've always relied upon protection from higher beings of light. Lady Faith teaches you to have total trust in the power of your own light.

Together, these angels are the keepers of the Sword of Truth. They're affiliated to the Throat chakra and will help you to use wise words when having uncomfortable honest discussions. Their etheric portal is the mountains of Banff, Canada.

Archangel Michael

Archangel Michael is dubbed the Prince of Angels, but I'd say that the 'King of Angels' is a more suited title. Archangel Michael, 'He who is like God', is probably the planet's most beloved and best-known angel. It's little wonder, for he's served humanity since the beginning of time. His amazingly strong and powerful energy sweeps into your sphere immediately upon your calling him. He makes you feel confident when you're nervous and safe when you're afraid. He's the ultimate angel of protection. If you ever get in over your head, he'll bail you out. He's truly fearless.

I recommend that all mediums, psychics, energy healers and carers invoke his protection each morning and night. He'll ensure your energy is impenetrable from the dark forces.

When you first begin to work with Archangel Michael, he often lets you know that he's around by the iconic white feather, or small blue flashing lights in your vision. He's a bit of a shapeshifter and has also appeared to me in the form of a robin from time to time, as he knows that they hold personal significance to me.

Like I said earlier, Archangel Michael has such a great sense of humour that he'll give you clairvoyant visions that'll have you in stitches. He's so funny and lights up the atmosphere with his jokes. He has a very strong relationship with Jesus and they developed quite the bond in His last incarnation. So, don't be surprised if they pop in together and check in on you when you're engaging in your spiritual activities.

Working with Lady Faith

When I'm working on a ritual or ceremony with Lady Faith, I create an altar to act as a physical focal point and to help to preserve the incoming energy that she brings through. I use a dark blue or purple altar cloth and blue or white candles, and I burn cedarwood essential oil.

Lady Faith's Gemstones

The following crystals have the healing vibrations that resonate with the work of Lady Faith:

- blue lace agate

- celestite

- sodalite

- lapis lazuli

- amethyst

- chrysocolla

By holding or wearing the listed gemstones you can strengthen your energetic connection to Lady Faith. They'll also help you with any issues you may have with self-expression or imbalances with the Throat chakra.

INVOCATION: CALLING IN LADY FAITH

For this next exercise, set aside some time to get to know Lady Faith. You may wish to set up a small altar using some of the items suggested earlier.

You will need:

~ a white candle

~ matches

~ incense of your choice

~ a pen and a piece of paper

When you're ready to begin, start by lighting your incense and candle:

~ Gently close your eyes.

~ Take a deep breath in through the nose and out through the mouth.

~ Placing your hands into the prayer position, say, 'Lady of Faith, Lady Faith, Lady Faith.'

~ Feel her strong and uplifting energy wash over you as she connects with you by standing by your side.

~ Her deep-blue energy begins to shroud you in every direction, strengthening your aura like a shield.

~ She draws a golden sword with a blazing blue flame from behind her back.

~ Holding the sword on its side, she kneels in front of you.

~ She asks if you're ready to bear the Sword of Truth.

~ If you're committed to becoming ever purer and truer, take the sword.

~ Bowing your head slightly, state: 'I accept the Sword of Truth, in my mind, in my body and in my soul. I accept the Sword of Truth. With this, I am whole.'

~ Now, imagine the sword shrinking down to about 5 centimetres (2 inches) in size.

~ Press the miniature sword upon your Throat chakra.

~ The blue flame of the tiny sword infuses its energy with your Throat chakra, giving you an additional blessing.

~ Feel the positive emotions of confidence and self-trust building within you.

~ Trust any visions or messages that come to you at this time.

~ Write down your experience.

~ Take a deep breath in through the nose and exhale loudly through the mouth, emitting an 'ahhh' sound.

~ Give thanks to Lady Faith.

~ Enjoy your day speaking words of wisdom and having faith in yourself.

You can invoke the sword's guidance if ever you need to uncover the truth, to exercise honesty and so you can act with integrity. Each time you connect to Lady Faith, she'll shed light on circumstances surrounding you to enable you to make a sound judgement.

The following exercise will allow you to call upon Archangel Michael's energy for psychic protection and emergency back-up. Once you understand energy-shielding basics and have gained in confidence, feel free to move on to the more advanced shielding exercise that follows in this chapter under the instruction of Lady Faith. This is my all-time favourite angel invocation. Go for it – you can dive right in with this one!

ARCHANGEL MICHAEL'S SHIELD OF PROTECTION

I recommend that you perform this exercise each morning and night before practising any meditations or rituals. If you feel under threat at any point in time, recite the invocation immediately. Remember, if in a panic you can always say 'Archangel Michael, help me,' and that will suffice!

~ Bringing your awareness to your feet, press your toes and heels into the ground beneath you.

~ Imagine clear quartz crystal roots shooting out of your soles, wriggling and twisting as they make their descent deep into the core of Mother Earth to ground and support you.

~ Now, call in Archangel Michael.

~ With your hands in the prayer position, say, 'Archangel Michael, Archangel Michael, Archangel Michael.'

~ Visualize this mighty Archangel stood in front of you with his flaming blue sword and golden shield of light.

~ Recite three times: 'Under your wings I stand, protected by God's first hand. From every direction shield me. In your light and love please seal me.'

~ Imagine Archangel Michael's sword touching the top of your aura and allow him to 'knight' you into his legions of the angels of the blue ray for protection.

~ As he does so, cobalt-blue light streams out from the tip of the sword and seals every inch of your aura.

~ Once your aura feels fully absorbed in Archangel Michael's light, allow it to flood into your chakras, protecting each of your inner gateways.

~ It's safe to leave the roots out beneath your feet, as they'll help you to remain grounded throughout the day.

~ Equally, feel free to visualize drawing them back in should you feel more comfortable doing so.

~ Thank Archangel Michael and go about your day.

You'll be totally safe to practise all of your inner work and rituals under the protection of Archangel Michael. He'll take anyone under his wings who calls him in.

The following exercise is designed to help you to develop an even greater strength to your energy field. By practising it each day, eventually you'll find you no longer require angels or Masters to protect you. You'll be fully equipped to do this for yourself.

Bear in mind that it does take a lot of repetition in order to build your internal power, the reason being that energy can be lost or altered in an instant. All it takes is a powerfully charged emotion to disrupt all of your hard work, which is why regular practice is imperative to maintain a solid matrix.

Archangel Michael will always fight your battles for you where he can, but Lady Faith will toughen you up. She'll make a spiritual warrior out of you yet!

BUILDING YOUR OWN PSYCHIC SHIELDS

Ensure that you've cleared the space in which you are practising by passing a burning herb bundle around you, by creating a sacred circle, or by burning cleansing frankincense essential oil nearby.

~ Sit with your feet flat on the floor and your spine straight.

~ Invoke Lady Faith.

~ With your hands in the prayer position, say, 'Lady Faith, Lady Faith, Lady Faith.'

~ Then state: 'I trust in my Divine power, upon myself, I call this hour, my sacred flame ignite, fuelled by my will, strength and might. In faith I am sealed, in faith I am healed, in faith and trust I am.'

~ Slow the pace of your breathing.

~ Place your hand on your belly and breathe deeply so that you can physically feel your hand rise and fall with each breath.

~ Now relax as Lady Faith touches each of your chakras with her radiant blue sword.

~ As she does so, visualize each chakra become sealed in an orb of cobalt-blue light.

~ Now, place a protective symbol (cross/om) of your choice over each orb to reinforce the protection.

~ Next, see the mini orbs covering your chakras merge into a mighty one.

~ This huge orb grows outwards, covering your aura entirely.

~ You're now fully cloaked in a sphere of blue light.

~ Feel the courage and the strength of your holy blue light.

~ Close your chakras one by one by watching them shut like doors, or like petals on flowers.

~ Thank Lady Faith for holding the space for your practice.

~ When you're ready, open your eyes.

~ Move about to ground your energy.

~ Thinking about your orb throughout the day will strengthen it even further.

This exercise will build your spiritual power. If you want to test your powers, experiment by not invoking external protection occasionally. Have Lady Faith on guard just in case. You'll be spiritually solid in no time!

Protecting Your Home

If your guardian angels can't get through to you, Lady Faith will always give you signs in the physical world to let you know when psychic shields are either down or if they've been invaded! This has happened to me many times over the years and if I wasn't on the lookout, I could have easily missed them.

When my drum beater began falling apart during a ceremony, I took it as an alert that an unwanted presence was about to attempt to breach my sacred space. Of course, being an avid believer that everything means something, I knew what the message meant, so I immediately strengthened my circle and called for assistance.

Other more subtle warning signs that I've received have been:

- knocking an angel statue on the floor, smashing its halo

- an invasion of ants in my home

- my Facebook page being hacked

- an attack from a person on social media, for sharing another person's business page

- crystals breaking

- people advertising their businesses in the comments of my blogs, feeding off my energy

- the handle falling off the back door

It's true that these types of incidents can just be 'one of those things', but when they do occur, just test your energy, as it's worth double-checking.

Here are some additional tips that you can use to protect your home from energy invaders, both physical and non-physical:

- Place a chunk of black tourmaline in each corner of the house.

- Hang an Egyptian ankh or a cross inside the house.

- Place a cast-iron horseshoe or an iron nail above the threshold.

- Stash an iron nail in each of your curtains to protect the windows.

- Grow herbs in pots on your windowsills.

- Plant lavender by the gate.

- Dispose of horror movies or books.

- Perform regular energy sweeps with smoke from your herb bundles.

- Prayer and chanting.

- Invoke the blue ray angels daily to stand at each direction of the house, including under the floor and over the roof.

- Cover up mirrors in the bedroom at night-time.

- Burn essential oils such as cedarwood and frankincense.

These handy tips are easy to implement and they'll help to strengthen your shields from all beings, including people who bring unwanted drama to your door.

Remember, the ancient Babylon texts state that cleanliness is next to godliness. Therefore, always attend to clearing your aura. This plays a major part in maintaining a good level of psychic protection.

Lady Faith is a wonderful ally to have by your side while you grow into a walking warrior of light. She'll shadow you as you reclaim all of your gifts and talents. Learn to trust in your own capabilities. Believe in yourself – you were born for this!

CHAPTER 7

Lady Haniel
Grace of the Goddess

I absolutely adore the magical Archeia Haniel. Think of her as being the angelic high priestess of a Sacred Feminine Mystery School. She carries within her all of the lost wisdom of the old ways from the times of the past when women knew that they were magical creatures and openly celebrated their divinity.

As you can probably imagine from the vibe of this book, Lady Haniel is one of the most revered light beings in my etheric girl gang. I can't imagine ever getting bored of working with her. She's fresh, edgy and exciting to be around. As she becomes more familiar within society, I'm certain that she'll become a favourite among the witches and priestesses, and within Goddess and nature-based worship.

The name Haniel means 'Grace', which is a feminine quality of compassion, humility and trust. She can help you to develop these virtues and with the power of grace, you'll learn to glide through life like a beautiful swan, appearing poised on the exterior even if your feet are paddling away for dear life beneath you. She's the angel of illusions and can help you to see right through people of low integrity and dishonesty.

Lady Haniel is the angel of all things associated with feminine energy such as intuition, the moon, magic, emotions, nurturing, birthing, shedding and creating. Her earthly roles that I'm highlighting within this book include teaching dreamtime skills such as lucid dreaming, reinitiating you into women's wisdom and showing you how to cycle with the moon.

Lady Haniel's Appearance

Lady Haniel appears to me as if she's from the faerie realm. She has a fresh, vibrant face with slender, pointy features, and she always has a cheeky glint in her big blue eyes. She has long platinum blonde hair that has an aura of its own! It glows subtly in her pale blue aura, as do her brilliant-white wings. She appears to me wearing long, floaty white dresses, but what really stands out is her amazing silver belt, which is decorated with the phases of the moon. She has a matching cuff over her left wrist and around her neck she wears a little moonstone pendant. Like a lot of women I know, she sure does like her bling.

Lady Haniel is very much connected to the unicorns and it's likely that she'll be accompanied by at least one when she comes through. If my clients have needed cleansing on a really deep level then the unicorns in her service have helped out by using their Third Eye spiral 'horn' of light to blitz through stubborn, dense energy, transforming down to the cellular structures of one's makeup.

Some of the myths of the Unicorn Tapestries contain the stories and legends of how these sacred beings would purify and bless our waters. They're pretty much back here today in the non-physical form to support Earth and her waters once again. As we're mainly made up of water, it makes sense that these sentient beings can have such a positive and life-changing influence over us, too.

Lady Haniel's Energy

Lady Haniel is very calming to be around, but as she's so closely connected to the moon and the element of Water, don't be surprised if unexpressed emotions come to the surface when you're working with her. You may find your energy purges through the shedding of gentle tears, but she'll remain with you when you're feeling down or depressed. You'll always feel relieved, lighter and clearer if this occurs.

Lady Haniel will hold you in a compassionate embrace and allow you to express your true feelings in a place free from judgement. She reminds us that 'it's better out than in'.

It comes as no surprise that in the Tarot she's represented by The Moon card. She's the queen of the night and illuminates things that we may prefer to avoid looking at. She's the angel to call upon when you doubt a person's loyalty or are feeling suspicious. She'll bring all frenemies and deceptive people to light.

She can help you with:

- developing intuition
- guiding you through shadow work
- clearing menstrual issues
- weeding out liars
- uncovering the truth
- cleansing and balancing your emotions
- understanding your own cycles

- developing a rhythm with the universe

- creating ceremonies

- manifesting wishes

- conjuring magic

- banishing negative energy

- increasing self-empowerment

- healing the Sacral chakra

- activating the Causal chakra

- meeting your unicorn

- hosting women's gatherings

- banishing insomnia

Lady Haniel's Calling Cards

As with all Archeiai, Lady Haniel has unique calling cards that help you to recognize her energy and to hear her call.

- Her number vibration is 10 – the number that signifies new beginnings on the horizon, as well as the endings and completion of cycles.

- Lady Haniel's animals are wolves and swans. Wolves are the animal totem of the moon and of the pack (our tribe). Swans represent her purity, connection to water and her grace. Her etheric companion is the unicorn.

- You may feel emotions rise to the surface when she's close by. Tears of joy are also common.

- You may notice an increase in your intuition and you may experience very vivid dreams after calling her in.

- Her flowers are moonflower and evening primrose – flowers that choose to face the light even when they're in the dark.

Angel of the Moon

Archeia Haniel is the angel of the moon. As we know, the moon has a massive influence upon our personal and collective energies. We've all heard the stories of people 'losing it' during a full moon, hence the word lunatic. You may also have been cautioned that results can take time when the moon is void of course. With our lives being so closely affected by the influence of the moon, it makes perfect sense that familiarizing yourself with her cycle would be of great benefit, even an ally, to you.

Lady Haniel says that we don't need to study this topic in depth. Being armed with the basics is enough to align you with this powerful Goddess lunar power. Lady Haniel says:

My loves, just as your moon affects the ebb and flow of the tides you, too, feel her impact on an individual level as you fluctuate and transition through each lunar cycle. To make the most of these phases you must become one with the cycles of nature. Gather your ideas and set intentions during the new moon. Sow and infuse them in the full moon, and release and let go in the waning moon.

This is a very simple yet incredibly powerful way to live in tune with life. Things just seem to fall into place when you work in sync with nature's rhythms. Everything in nature is cyclic, just like you. If you're female, then your energy and your menstrual cycles – if applicable – will coincide with the eight phases of the moon, hence the term 'moontime'. Men are attuned to the eight longer annual solar cycles.

By consciously aligning your energy – or menstrual cycle – with the phases of the moon you gain additional opportunities to better understand and know yourself. You'll discover where your perfect windows of timing lie to plant, pause, reap or end. Lady Haniel urges you to grab your diary, google the current moon phase and map out these optimal timings for you as an individual. For example, I'd never begin a new diet regime two days before my moontime or on the cusp of the full moon. This is because it would potentially be setting myself up for failure, as during these periods my emotions are heightened, making me more inclined to give in to comfort food.

The optimal time for me to embark on a detox would be either the onset of the new moon or just after my moontime, when I have energy that's more vibrant and I'm mentally ready for a challenge. There's a perfect time for everything.

Lunar Tips

You probably already know that placing your crystals out under a full moon will charge them up with beams of energy, but have you tried moon bathing yourself? It's really simple and really magical.

During the next full moon, take a yoga mat outside and wrap up warm. If the moon is visible, lie back and face her; if not, use your imagination. Visualize silver light streaming down into your body and filling you with her wisdom from head to toe. This process will supercharge your intuition and connect you more deeply to your mystical side.

You can also use the light from the full moon as an opportunity to make some moon shine water: moon-blessed water that you can use to sprinkle about over your crystals or over your altar, or even to drink to make a toast at the end of a ceremony or ritual.

To make your moon shine, use a glass jug and fill it with spring water. Leave it on a window ledge – or outside if you're brave enough! – on the night of the full moon or a day either side. Remember to set an intention by placing your hands over the water. Here are a few words that I like to say to bless it, which has helped me to manifest unbelievable opportunities:

Lady Moon, Lady Night, Lady Haniel, I claim your light. Imprint this water with your wisdom bright to see me through the darkest night. The wishes I make upon this eve are now made manifest, already achieved. And so it is.

The full moon is mostly a magical time, yet on occasion it can be uncomfortable. This is because if we consistently fail to look at our problems then there's nothing like a full moon or an eclipse to bring things to a head.

Some people suffer from mild physical symptoms, too. If you tend to suffer with headaches or insomnia during full or supermoons, then ask Lady Haniel to place her blue pyramid of light over your Third Eye chakra before bed. This will filter out extra-strong moonbeams that may be uncomfortable for you. Placing an amethyst crystal under your pillow also helps.

Angel Encounter

I first met Lady Haniel about 20 years ago. I simply stumbled across her name on the internet and I was intrigued to know more about this mysterious angel whom I'd never met. Of course, online it referred to Archeia Haniel as being masculine, so I was pleasantly surprised when during the invocation 'she' came in.

For about 10 years she fluctuated throughout my life, often making an appearance when I was healing women who were suffering from women's issues. She'd give me suggestions for simple remedies, oils, crystals or vitamins that could be of benefit for the woman's individual needs.

As I got older, I began to remember the magic of the womb portal and I was hungry to learn more. That's when Lady Haniel's visits became more frequent. Together with Lady Hope, she showed me past-life visions of me participating in womb-healing rituals while serving as a priestess of Isis. The angels encouraged me to start incorporating the sacred ceremonies and blessings into my therapies and workshops. They proved to be very successful in helping women to release energy of past sexual partners, shame, sexual abuse and loss.

Archeia Haniel is now one of my favourite angels. She's brought to the surface many treasures from the depths of my soul. What precious gems of wisdom are dormant within you? Meditate with her and pray to her for guidance, and she'll help you to uncover your jewels. She says that everything you need is right there, inside you.

Angel of Women's Rites

Lady Haniel sometimes works with Lady Hope. They're both keepers of different aspects of women's wisdom. As I mentioned earlier, Lady Haniel helps women with menstrual issues, whereas Lady Hope will offer support around fertility and pregnancy.

Lady Haniel is also a ceremonialist. She rejoices when we mark the change in seasons and when we're initiated into rites of passage – a lovely tradition that's been lost among the modernization of the ages.

As a woman, your first rite of passage is marked by the first menstrual cycle (menarche). The wise women, the crones, those who honour the magic and mystery not just in women but in life itself, would be the ones to initiate girls into womanhood. They did this with celebratory rituals and anointment. In some traditions a woman would be initiated into the Red Tent, a place where she would rest and scry for visions and guidance when the veils between worlds are most thin.

Lady Haniel points out the importance of honouring your body through rites of passage. She says that in our process of evolution and change, rites help us to accept who and where we are. It helps us to embrace our purpose. A woman initiated into the motherhood rites finds it much easier to let go of her career to embrace this stage in her life – pregnancy – because she knows it's temporary. She feels as though she has permission to focus on her current purpose of raising a child without having to excel in work at the same time.

I always remember my GP scorning me when I told her how exhausted I was during pregnancy. She remarked how she'd worked right up until the day before she'd given birth and returned two weeks later. I felt like a failure, not being able to juggle things efficiently. Had I been initiated as I crossed the threshold into motherhood, I may have had less expectation of myself. Second time round I surrendered to pregnancy, taking each day as it came, counting my blessings as opposed to ticking off the to-do list.

Another aspect of change we've been conditioned to fear is ageing. We're taught to try to delay this process of evolving into our wise woman self – the most revered aspect of womanhood in ancient traditions. But what if instead of feeling depressed about the arrival of grey hairs, we welcomed them? How liberating would it feel if rather than dyeing your hair you showed off your silver locks that have been moonstruck with the wisdom of the grandmothers?

In sacred feminine wisdom there are four typical rites of passage:

- Maidenhood – first menses

- Motherhood – first pregnancy

- Enchantress – explorer/wild woman

- Crone – menopause (moon pause)

Because the priestesses and wise women had to go underground, as women we now find ourselves with no heritage. Unless you're exceptionally lucky, you probably have no elders bestowing you with your ancestral wisdom or to look up to for guidance. However, your circumstances can still enable you to reclaim these teachings. The angels can be your guides, as they have been for me.

We're the generation who is instigating massive change. We're the founders of a new golden heritage that will serve our daughters, to ensure that they're empowered with the wisdom that we never received. If this kind of talk gives you goose bumps, if it ignites a fire in your soul, then get to know Lady Haniel. She'll draw back the timelines so that you can access all of the knowledge that by birthright is yours.

Lady Haniel draws like-minded women together to educate and empower one another. She oversees development circles and moon lodges. She loves watching us mending our broken bonds and recreating our sisterhood. If you've been alone in your journey so far or are seeking 'more' from your current circles, call in Lady Haniel to align you with your spiritual tribe.

The Graceful Duo

Lady Haniel's twin flame counterpart is Archangel Nathaniel. They're closely connected with nature, but whereas Lady Haniel is the angel of above (the moon), Nathaniel is the angel of below (the Earth). She shows us how to tune in to our watery feelings. And Archangel Nathaniel will help us to clear them as we pull them from our thoughts and release or cleanse them using our bodies.

These angels are keepers of the light blue diamond ray. This fragment of God's light can be used to connect us to all of the moons in the universes. Their etheric portal is located at the Pyramid of the Moon, Mexico.

Archangel Nathaniel

Archangel Nathaniel is one of the lesser-known Archangels, although he's becoming increasingly more popular on Earth because of the growing mass awareness of the Law of Attraction. His name, meaning 'Gift of God' or 'God has Given', demonstrates his ability to find the gifts and blessings in all things.

He's one of the angels who can help you to attract opportunities, to bring more abundance into your life, and to feel happy and grateful for what you already have. He'll help you to manifest whatever you need to enable you to complete your life's mission, and he may also offer you insight into the next phase of your purpose.

When he visits me, Archangel Nathaniel wears a white-and-gold robe and his aura radiates a lovely turquoise blue colour. His shoulder-length hair is dark brown in colour. In looks, he reminds me of the famous Italian artist Leonardo da Vinci in his younger years.

Archangel Nathaniel lived life as John the Baptist. During that lifetime he demonstrated miracles and performed rebirthing ceremonies using the power of water. Water is a powerful gateway into other realms.

Archangel Nathaniel has such an affinity with water that he's one of the Archangels who has teams of angels who reside by waterfalls and wishing wells. They wait for us to share our dreams and to hear our prayers. He also watches over and guides the Brotherhood of Light, the masculine counterpart to the Sisterhood of the Rose. He helps men to express their emotions and encourages them to develop their feminine virtues. You can pray to Archangel Nathaniel if you're worried about a son or brother who's experiencing pressures or who's heavily subscribed to unrealistic expectations of what it is to be a man.

He takes a particular shine to the single dads, care providers and those mentally injured fighting in the service of others. Under the Law of Grace, it only takes a prayer from a loved one to allow Archangel Nathaniel to help our men who suffer in silence to find a shoulder to cry on. Together, Archangels Nathaniel (given) and Haniel (grace) become 'God has given Grace'.

Working with Lady Haniel

Archangel Haniel has magical correspondences to Monday (Moonday) – the Old English *Mōnandæg*, 'day of the moon' – making this potentially the most perfect day to perform a ritual with her. Her herb is mugwort, which you could drink as a tea or simply leave her a small piece as an offering upon your altar.

I always use a silver altar cloth for rituals with Lady Haniel and I offer her either blue, silver or white candles. There are many essential oils that you could burn to invoke her magic, such as orange, spearmint, frankincense or rose. Next is a list of crystals that can strengthen your connection to Lady Haniel and enable you to receive clearer guidance from her:

Lady Haniel's Gemstones

The following crystals have the healing vibrations that resonate with the work of Lady Haniel:

- moonstone

- rainbow moonstone

- selenite

- labradorite

- opal

- amethyst

- celestite

Use any of the listed gemstones to direct potent lunar energies to enhance any magical rituals and especially when exploring women's wisdom. You can access a deeper connection to Lady Haniel by wearing or holding any of these crystals.

 ## INVOCATION: CALLING IN LADY HANIEL

Lady Haniel is such a lovely angel to work with, especially if you already have an affinity with the moon.

You will need:

~ a simple white candle

~ if you wish, you can wear white or silver

~ peppermint essential oil is a good choice for your oil burner

~ a pen and a piece of paper

Here's an invocation that she provided me with to call in her loving, magical presence:

~ Light your candle.

~ With your hands in prayer position, whisper Lady Haniel's name three times.

~ Say, 'Lady Haniel, Lady Haniel, Lady Haniel.'

~ Imagine her stood in front of you now.

~ State, 'Lady Haniel, Priestess of the Moon, I call in your Divine presence now and ask that you align me with all of the wisdom that already lies within me. Thank you for opening the doorways that guard the inner dimensions of love and higher intelligence. I reawaken my channels to become once again a great conductor of light, and so it is.'

~ Placing your attention on your Causal chakra (above the Crown chakra), it begins to glow, resembling a tiny bright white full moon.

~ Lady Haniel takes a silver key from around her neck and inserts it into your Causal chakra.

~ As she turns the key, your moon gateway opens and pure, dazzling light rays begin to shine out into your aura.

~ These high-dimensional light rays uplift your energy bodies, enabling you to carry and channel higher frequencies of light.

~ Watch rainbow-coloured snowflakes begin to emerge from this gateway.

~ They gently float down and crystallize in your field.

~ The wisdom captured within these structures will thaw out into your consciousness as and when needed.

~ Lady Haniel places one of the snowflakes into your hands.

~ Rest your gaze upon the intricate patterns with the intention of receiving a message of wisdom from Lady Haniel; it may come as a word or an image.

~ Gently close the Causal chakra moon gate by visualizing it closing over.

~ Thank Lady Haniel.

~ Wiggle your fingers and toes to ground your awareness fully back into the here and now.

~ Take notes of your experience – you may wish to reflect on the notes in future.

Now that you've been initiated into Lady Haniel's energy, your intuition will develop at a pace that's perfect for you. She visits a lot of people in their dreams, especially around the time of the full moon. She'll help you to recall your dreams and decode the subconscious messages within them.

The following exercise is a really powerful technique to allow you to shed negative energy. Maybe you've been feeling down or perhaps you've collected another person's fears within your field – which is very common if you've been listening to people's worries and so forth – but the next exercise is sure to help:

SHEDDING NEGATIVITY DURING MOONTIME

This ritual is performed in conjunction with your moontime, or the dark moon phase if you don't bleed.

You will need:

~ a pen and a piece of paper

~ a black candle to banish or white candle to purify – whichever feels more appropriate

At the onset of your moontime or dark moon phase (search date online), answer these questions in relation to the last month:

~ Are you holding on to any unwanted anger?

~ Have you taken offence at anyone or anything?

~ Are you harbouring any hard feelings towards another person?

~ What negative thinking or criticism have you had about yourself?

~ If you've had sex, who was it with this month?

~ And if so, can you feel their energy in your womb space?

~ Is there anybody else who's draining your womb space energy? Trust that whoever first comes to mind is the right one you need to work with.

~ What are you ready to release?

Once you have your list, light your candle.

~ Call in Lady Haniel by placing your hands into a prayer posture and whisper or sing her name three times.

~ Say, 'Lady Haniel, Lady Haniel, Lady Haniel.'

~ Go outside – or look out from a window – and face the moon if it's visible.

~ Place your hand over your Sacral chakra and recite: 'With the moontime I am aligned with the powers of She, with nature both within and without me. I am ready to release [reel off the answers from your list] and all negativity I carry both consciously and unconsciously.'

~ Exercising caution, burn the list with the candle flame.

~ Smash the candle or allow it to burn down (without leaving it unattended for safety reasons), then dispose of it outside of your home.

~ Placing your hands in prayer position, look up and give thanks to Lady Haniel.

For the next two nights continue strengthening your releasing ritual by going outside for just a few minutes each evening. Looking up towards the moon, place your hands over the Sacral chakra and recite the decree once again. Visualize the flame burning your list. I've seen some fabulous results with this exercise over the years. When in tune with the moon, we women are oh-so magical.

~

Lucid Dreaming

Lucid dreaming is the ability to be conscious within a dream. It's a practice that many new age seekers will dabble in at some point – and so they should! Lucid dreaming is a whole lot of fun. Imagine being 'awake' and consciously able to participate within the creation process of your dream! Lady Haniel, the Queen of the Night, is the perfect angel to teach you to master this technique while safely under her protection.

Lucid dreaming is the ultimate spiritual playground, and in addition to the fun and games, there are also healing benefits to be attained from consciously exploring the non-physical dreamworld. Lucid dreaming is different from astral travel, as you can astral travel without being aware of doing so. To remember the journey you need to remain lucid. During dreamtime we all travel to other dimensions and journey through realms. This isn't unique to those on the path. On our night-time travels we acquire spiritual knowledge from teachers, Ascended Masters, ancestors, guides and star beings.

This is when we may also visit the Archangels in their retreats to receive their wisdom. All of this sounds just fabulous, but we need to commit to morning meditations to download the teachings in order to integrate them into our waking lives, so the wisdom remains embedded in the subconscious mind.

It's like going to university all of your life and never once applying the knowledge. Potentially, you could be wasting spiritual intelligence by not tapping in to it. If you never master the art of lucid dreaming that's okay – you can still access data from silent meditation.

During my time studying shamanic practices, I was initiated into the teachings of plant medicines, one of which was Lady Mugwort – the inducer of lucid dreaming. Like the angels, Lady Mugwort is a living consciousness and she can grant you access into the magical state of dreaming awake.

Lady Haniel would love to accompany you on your journey. She'll protect you and help you to develop the practice, as it takes patience to develop. It doesn't usually come overnight (pun intended).

As mentioned, lucid dreaming differs from astral travel. The steps in this exercise are designed to enhance your ability to become conscious. However, as we all astral travel during sleep, the first time you become lucid you may well panic! This is totally normal as you get used to being conscious as a non-physical being.

If you do panic during a lucid dream and want to force yourself to wake, you must connect to your physical body by focusing on it. When I was younger I would sometimes become afraid at the sight of my body lying in the bed below me. Another time I freaked out when I became conscious and my spirit was somehow down the side of my bed – you sure can get in some peculiar places when you're not lugging around a physical body! I shared my concerns with an old yogi I knew, and he told me to focus on my big toe if I wanted to come back in an emergency. Strangely enough, it absolutely works!

LUCID DREAM JOURNEY

This exercise is intended to be performed just before you go to sleep, to induce a state of lucid dreaming and to strengthen your chances of recalling regular dreams. You can work with Lady Haniel every night if you're interested in dreamwork, but keep Lady Mugwort for special occasions. The potent effects of the mugwort could be lost on you should you use it too often. The full moon is a particularly potent time to induce a lucid dream. This is when the veils between the conscious and subconscious are uber thin and psychic abilities are heightened.

Please consult a medical practitioner before working with herbs if you're taking any medications, you're pregnant or if you have a serious health concern.

You will need:

~ mugwort herbal tea or tincture

~ an offering to Lady Mugwort such as a crystal, a biscuit or some tobacco

~ lavender oil (diluted to the ratio of 2 drops to 10 ml of carrier oil such as grapeseed oil)

~ a white candle

~ a dried herb bundle to burn

~ a silver or white shawl or cloth (optional)

~ a pen and a piece of paper

First, prepare your tea or tincture. Always follow instructions for dosage as they differ between brands. Then take it to bed along with the other items required.

~ Lay down your cloth in your bedroom and place all of your magical items upon it.

~ Light your herb bundle and blow the smoke over your items to bless them.

~ Say, 'In the name of light and love, these items are blessed and filled with the highest Divine light.'

~ Light your candle in the name of Lady Haniel by saying, 'Lady Haniel, Lady Haniel, Lady Haniel, I call upon your Divine presence now. Please assist me in creating a sacred space where only love may enter.'

~ Place a drop of the lavender oil upon the Third Eye chakra (brow) and on the centre of the soles of each foot to activate your clear vision and to protect you as you walk between worlds.

~ Holding the teacup or tincture bottle in your hands, sit with your spine straight.

~ Set your intention by stating aloud, 'Tonight I will lucid dream,' or 'In the morning I will remember my dreams.'

~ Slowly drink half or all of the tea or take the tincture while focusing on your intention.

~ For safety reasons, now blow out your candle.

~ Turn off the lights and climb into bed.

~ Lying on your back, take three really deep breaths in through your nose and out through your mouth, really opening up your chest and belly.

~ Now, see Lady Haniel cradling your head in her gentle hands.

~ One hand is placed upon your forehead and the other gently supports your occipital area (base of the skull).

~ Her blue-ish glow relaxes you deeply.

~ Try to 'feel' the presence of Lady Mugwort travelling through your body.

~ Her green light emanates from the ingested tea, spreading a healing green glow as she travels through your body.

~ Lady Haniel brings in Lady Mugwort to meet you.

~ She looks like a beautiful green goddess and she smiles lovingly at you.

~ She takes your hand and agrees to open the gateways to allow you to experience a lucid dream journey.

~ Lady Haniel will accompany you all night long in a loving embrace.

~ If you want to travel somewhere specific then share your wishes now.

~ Now, go to sleep.

~ Upon waking – even if it's still night – take out the pen and paper and say aloud, 'I remember my dreams and travels.'

~ Write down everything that comes to mind; even if it's only a few fragments, it'll increase over time.

If you were successful in having a lucid dream, then you'll have become aware that you were dreaming and will have had some degree of control over the experience. For example, if you thought of Tutankhamun in a lucid dream then in an instant you would have been in his tomb, seen his mask or similar. Everything happens instantaneously.

Tips for Remembering Your Dreams

The word 'remember' means to piece things back together. All of the information is buried deep within you. Lady Haniel will help you to piece back the memories that are within your subconscious mind. To be 're-membered' is to be placed back together – to become whole in mind, body and spirit.

- Have a pen and a piece of paper by the bed.

- Set an anchor (a reminder) by the side of the bed to help you to get into the habit of jotting down memories immediately upon waking. This could simply be leaving a pen and a notepad headed 'Last night I dreamed...', prompting you to answer the question.

- Meditation with Lady Haniel will slowly awaken your dream skills.

- Place amethyst or moonstone crystals under your pillow.

- Practice, practice, practice.

Lady Haniel is one of the angels who can help you to sharpen your intuition. Combine her healing energy with the feminine potency of the moon and your clairvoyance can be supercharged. It's useful to note that some phases of the moon can actually distort our perceptions, making it difficult to differentiate when our instincts are on form or when we've been influenced by external powers.

The trick to combat this oversight is to finely tune your connection to your own cycle. Try the following exercise to track your internal moon calendar:

ACTIVATE YOUR LUNAR POWERS

This next exercise is best practised throughout an entire moon cycle:

~   Find the date of the upcoming new moon.

~   Set the date in your diary and on this night go outside.

~   Facing the moon, call in Lady Haniel by speaking her name three times.

~   Say, 'Lady Haniel, Lady Haniel, Lady Haniel.'

~   You see Lady Haniel travelling down towards you.

~   She wraps you in her white wings.

~   She gently tilts your face towards the sky and beckons to the moon.

~   Silvery, shimmering moonbeams begin to stream down.

~   See them directly entering your Third Eye chakra.

~   A beautiful indigo rose begins to stir within your Third Eye as the moonlight penetrates this chakra.

~   Fill yourself with this powerful feminine light.

~   When you're ready, close down the flower by visualizing the petals folding inwards, the bud securely locking in the door of your Third Eye chakra.

~   Raise your hands to the sky and give thanks to both Lady Haniel and the energies of the new moon.

Do this every night for the next 28 days. Your findings will help you to become in tune with your own rhythm and that of the moon.

~

Lady Haniel is a great teacher to work with. She'll deepen all of your current spiritual practices and administer you with additional knowledge to help you along the path back to nature and self-realization. She'll teach you about cycles and optimal timings to embark upon or release projects.

CHAPTER 8

Lady Hope
Wish of the Goddess

Lady Hope is a wonderful uplifting angel who's always full of the joys of spring. I absolutely love working with her, especially when I need that extra burst of inspiration to keep me strongly focused on a project. Just saying her name out loud elevates your spirit, triggering a spark of 'hope' within you.

Being the angel of wishes, she invites you to contemplate what would make your life more fulfilling. She'll help you to make the inner assessments that lead you to discover what your soul is calling for. Then, she'll walk you through the steps of what's required to bring your dream to life.

Have you noticed the huge rise in ambitious and self-made people across the planet? This number has increased dramatically and continues to do so as human consciousness rises and people step up to reclaim their power. In 2013, Archeia Hope enveloped Earth with her high-vibrational light, called the Cloak of Optimism, seeding her inspirational energy into the collective. This triggered a mass awakening of self-belief, which naturally created a ripple effect, leading others to catch on to the wave of aspiration. You can call upon this light to ignite any area of your life.

Even more excitingly, you can use it to create a whole new way of thinking. Lady Hope's Cloak of Optimism can be intentionally programmed to fire loopholes in your old thought patterns, rewiring your brain to higher states of awareness. This is essential in developing an unlimited consciousness.

Lady Hope and her legions of white ray angels have been assigned many duties at this time on Earth. In this chapter, we'll be studying how these angels can help you to:

- tap in to Lady Hope's optimistic energy, inspiring you to create your best life
- enter the void of creation to seed your wishes
- rediscover the lore of the womb

Lady Hope's Appearance

Lady Hope is very beautiful. She has the most amazing bright white aura that twinkles with flashes of gold and green. Because she's so high vibrational, she appears to be the most ethereal of all the angels, which is also a reflection of her deep purity.

When she visits me, she wears a simple white gown, but if you look closely, embroidered on it is a very delicate fleur-de-lis (French for lily flower) pattern. Her sleek hair is a light golden colour, which makes her dark green eyes stand out in contrast. She carries a golden sceptre with the fleur-de-lis sitting proudly on the top. The fleur-de-lis has lots of spiritual symbolism attached to it, which we'll explore further on in this chapter.

Lady Hope's Energy

Lady Hope is very much the archetypal Empress in the Tarot deck. She generously spills out blessings of abundance and fertility from her overflowing cup of love wherever she goes. She's governed by the element of Water, which heralds her feminine associations to purification, emotions, creativity, the womb and feminine magic.

When you're working with her, you're likely to feel giddy and excited like a child. She stirs your soul, compelling you to delve deep into exploration of your true passions. Creativity is enhanced, and all kinds of ideas and epiphanies come to mind. This makes her the perfect angel to call upon if you're an artist or a writer.

Lady Hope can also be thought of as the fairy godmother of the Archeiai. However, in addition to granting you wishes, she also teaches you to reclaim your crown by becoming cocreator with the Divine. Just like a coach, she'll support you with step-by-step guidance, magically enabling you to attract love, abundance and opportunities into your reality.

She can help you with:

- giving birth to ideas

- heightening creativity

- adjusting to pregnancy

- maintaining balance during menstruation

- accessing your blueprint of potential

- creating a life of miracles

- manifesting abundance

- facilitating purification rituals

- understanding wake-up calls

- tuning in to inspiration

- enhancing motivation

- making your wishes come true

- becoming hopeful and optimistic

- daring to dream bigger

- healing the womb centre

- nurturing yourself and others

- changing your thinking

- becoming a believer

Lady Hope's Calling Cards

Like all of the female Archangels, Lady Hope has her own bespoke calling cards to help you to recognize her presence:

- The number sequence 333 is associated with Lady Hope. It's the number of Christ Consciousness and also the Holy Trinity. Seeing these digits can herald the arrival of a third party, such as a baby, or even the homecoming of your own soul as the Divine child.

- Lady Hope's animals are cranes. These birds denote good luck and are particularly helpful when working with mothers to achieve balance in work and home life. After starting to work with her, you may see one on a nature programme, or you may even be sitting on the train when you notice someone with a crane tattoo. This would be a clear sign that she's near.

- You may feel the urge to write something like a poem or words of wisdom without knowing where they're coming from.

- You may feel inspired to engage in an artistic project that's connected to your soul path – or by engaging in the project itself you realize your soul path!

- Your Sacral chakra can buzz or tingle with energy.

- Lady Hope's flower is the lily. This trumpet-like flower depicts messages that come from God/dess or the angels. You may be given a bunch of these flowers or simply see them on a card. Alternatively, you may even see the fleur-de-lis symbol.

The Fleur-de-Lis

The lily flower is a very common symbol. You're probably familiar with it displayed upon coats of arms and flags, but it also holds many deeply spiritual meanings.

The fleur-de-lis

First and foremost, I think it's safe to say that it's always been used as a representation of communication with angels. The most famous messenger angel of all time being Lady Hope's twin ray, Archangel Gabriel. Lilies frequently appear in artwork next to this Archangel, the most famous painting being the *Annunciation* by da Vinci.

Another facet of the fleur-de-lis is in how its three petals represent the trifold flame of the higher heart centre (your angelic heart) that resides close to the thymus (slightly higher than the Heart chakra). Each of your spiritual flames awaken when you aspire to become angelic yourself. This is attained by becoming the physical embodiment of the three virtues: Faith, Hope and Charity.

Lady Charity stands for the archetypal maiden and the pink flame. Lady Hope represents the pure white flame and archetypal mother. Lady Faith holds the blue flame representing the wise crone.

The fleur-de-lis is also associated with St Joseph, father of Yeshua. It symbolized the protection that Lady Hope and Archangel Gabriel gave him as he reared the young Jesus.

The fleur-de-lis is loaded with symbolism. Another take on it weaves in the repression of women. In this legend, the fleur-de-lis represents a mermaid's tail; in turn representing the sleeping feminine wisdom residing in the depths of the ocean – the subconscious mind. Furthermore, the mermaid losing her voice once again speaks of the silencing and disempowering of women.

Angel of Hope

Lady Hope can help you to develop an optimistic outlook on life. We all know that your thoughts become your feelings and then those feelings manifest your life experiences, so positive thinking is essential to create a joyful and contented life.

The power of hope can create miracles! Hope is the magical energy that the Law of Attraction requires to deliver results. Without it, our wishes may not come to fruition. Being hopeful sends a message to the universe that you have faith. When you trust that all is well, you'll always be supported – that is spiritual law!

If you're feeling hopeless, have a health issue, are lonely or you can't pay your bills, then ask Lady Hope to inspire you. Sometimes it's too difficult to 'fake it till you make it'. After all, how can you 'feel' rich when you're having sleepless nights over your lack of finances? And how can you 'feel' well when you've been bedridden with sickness or pain?

This is where Lady Hope can come in handy. By allowing her energy to penetrate your mind, body and spirit, little bursts of hope ignite within every single cell of your body. With daily practice, you can eventually recalibrate your whole being. Miracles occur when you surrender your fears to Lady Hope and alchemize them into positivity.

Angel Encounter

Lady Hope is the angel of miracles. When I want to attract something seemingly difficult into my life, she's my first-choice angel to whom I offer up my prayers. I often retell the following story at my Law of Attraction manifesting workshops. It's inspiring to know that even against great odds, Lady Hope can make the impossible possible.

When my daughter was two years old, I spotted the most amazing little boots in the January sales. Despite the fact that the shop didn't have them available in her size, I still desperately wanted to buy them for her. They were super cute, in a limited-edition fuchsia pink with turquoise bows. They were to die for!

Back then, money was very tight, but in an impulse moment I hastily made the purchase all the same. Proud owner of the new boots, I smiled to myself as I tucked them into the wardrobe, stashing them away for the following winter.

Nine months later, I pulled the little beauties out of the box. But to my dismay, I immediately realized that something was very wrong. It turned out that both boots were for the left foot! After the initial sting of disappointment, I remembered that I still had the receipt.

I wondered if perhaps I could get an exchange, or if they still had the two right-footed boots in the stockroom.

Armed with kids and boots, I drove out of town, heading to the little boutique shop where I'd bought them. But once I reached there, I encountered yet another obstacle – the shop had closed down! I drove back home feeling a little deflated but not defeated. Bent on having them, I even called the supplier, who couldn't help me, either.

Later, my sister arrived and over coffee I described my fiasco. She was furious at the thought of me being ripped off. She ranted away about the stupidity of the shopkeeper and how unfair the situation was. Her ramblings began to fade into the distance as I removed my attention and went inwards to pray.

I called in Lady Hope and asked her for a miracle. I knew that in order to receive my miracle I'd need to shore up some faith, which wasn't the easiest of tasks. With all of the setbacks so far, I was beginning to struggle with doubts and feelings of being the victim.

Lady Hope answered my call immediately. Lovingly, she assured me that she'd help me to believe and that that would be enough to allow this situation to be resolved. I didn't know how, though, as it all seemed impossible at this point – a lost cause, even. Nevertheless, I always believe in the angels, so as she instructed, I let go of the situation. I had sent in my prayer request and there was nothing to do now but have faith.

A couple of weeks passed and nothing happened. No emails arrived to say, 'You won't believe it, we've found your boot!' Nor had I awoken to find elves fashioning me a right-footed boot from the material. Yet, the desire for a solution remained with me.

Then one morning during my daily meditation Lady Hope popped in. She told me to have a look for the boots on eBay. Bearing in mind these boots were like gold dust, I still did as she asked. Lo and behold, a seller had a pair, new in the box and exactly the same size! Momentarily, I thought *why should I have to buy them again?* But my doubt was soon overcome by a strong feeling of hope and gratitude. It was a miracle that I'd actually found a pair!

As I clicked the 'Buy it now' button for the second pair of boots that I couldn't really afford, I felt exhilarated. There was magic in the air.

A few days later the boots finally arrived. I sat my little girl down, excited for her to put them on, but was stunned to discover that both boots were right-footed. I now had two pairs of fuchsia pink UGG boots in the same size! I decided to call the seller; unusually, he'd inserted a thank-you note in the parcel, which included his phone number! It was as if the angels had everything covered. I rang him and went on to explain how he'd sent me two right-footed boots and that strangely, I had the matching two left-footed ones.

As we chatted away, I innocently mentioned the name of the boutique where I'd made my purchase. The seller began to laugh. Despite the fact that he lived more than 200 miles away from me, it was in fact the exact same shop where he'd bought his boots some nine months earlier. It turned out that they were too small for his daughter, so he, too, had put them aside and for some unknown reason, had hung on to them for nine months before deciding to sell them on eBay (not realizing they were unsuitable for wear). We made a compromise. I kept one of his boots and I sent him one of mine. He then gave me a refund. We were both happy now that we each had the correct pair.

Lady Hope had kept my energy high, enabling a window of opportunity to open up and allow me to receive. If I'd lost control over my emotions and allowed doubt and fear to creep in for too long, I'm certain that a totally different story would have unfolded, one without a happy ending.

How unbelievable is that story? The odds were stacked against me and yet miracle after miracle occurred in perfect timing in order to create a happy solution. If I ever doubt my ability to manifest something, I take a look at the photo of my daughter holding the two pairs of boots. Then I remind myself that if I can do that then I can do anything!

Next time you have a wish, no matter how unrealistic it may seem, just try calling in Lady Hope. She'll uplift your energy to the state necessary to draw your desire to you. Alternatively, she can take you straight to the Cosmic Womb, where you can withdraw the blueprint of your wish and nurture it to fruition by directing your own creative energies to support its growth. Your womb space can bring anything to life.

Angel of the Womb

Within each woman lies a magical portal. This portal is the womb space, which can be thought of as the microcosm of the great void of creation – the place where all things emanate and from which all of our ideas are born.

Lady Hope is one of the guardians who can assist you in reclaiming your heritage of womb wisdom. As I mentioned earlier, Lady Haniel governs the shedding and releasing aspects of the womb rites, while Archeia Hope aligns us to the manifesting side of these sacred feminine mysteries. They're both keepers of the ancient wisdom of the womb.

Womb magic has been used since the beginning of time. Even before bodies became physical in form, the womb gateway was encoded into our matrix. This meant that we could maintain a connection to the very life force of creation, enabling manifestations to quantum leap into our reality.

So, you see this kind of magic can be practised whether you have a physical womb or not, as the energetic womb centre is inherent within you. Humanity has been duped into the belief that women and wombs are only for making babies, but in truth the same sparks of creation that make a human life can be harvested to create anything. The womb is unlimited in what it births. By tapping in to your womb space, you can connect with the raw creative or destructive energies of the Goddess herself.

It isn't an accident that so little is known about the womb. After all, it's arguably the most powerful energy centre in the body. Within it lie reservoirs of knowledge – the entire secrets of creation. Lady Hope can help you to access this space to gain inspiration for ideas and to retrieve the blueprint of your wishes directly from the great Cosmic Mother.

Just take a moment to contemplate how amazing the physical womb is. This interdimensional portal is the only place in the world where the alchemy of spirits into human form takes place! If you're a woman, the gateway of life lies within your physical body!

With Lady Hope, you can use the womb space to:

- manifest wishes

- channel creative energies to paint or write

- express your sexuality

- tune in to the Goddess

- listen to your body – clairsentience

- assist in conception

- realize your desires

- harvest the energy to manifest your dreams

TUNE IN TO YOUR WOMB

There's a very simple mudra that you can practise right now if you're raring to get started with connecting to the womb. It's called the Yoni Mudra. When practised, the fingertips fire up an energetic circuit to the womb.

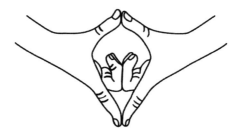

The Yoni Mudra

Holding this hand position for around 10 minutes connects you very deeply to your sacred silent womb portal. It tops your energy up with vibrant healing life force from the Cosmic Mother, awakening the sleeping feminine within you. Once you're familiar with the hand pose, then you're ready to try using it.

~ Either sitting or standing, keep your spine straight and take three deep breaths in through your nose and out through your mouth.

~ Place your fingers together as shown, thumb and first finger gently touching, roughly making a downward-pointing triangle shape.

~ The middle, index and little finger are bent inwards, resting upon each other from the knuckles.

~ Letting your hands rest gently a few inches above the womb area, concentrate on your breath and feel the energetic connection building between your fingertips.

~ Imagine a golden ball of light growing more intently in this area.

~ Enjoy this practice for as long as you like.

~ Afterwards, it's a good idea to spend or save the energy you've gathered.

~ Just like water in a vase, still energy becomes stagnant.

~ To build your personal power or for healing, simply imagine placing the ball of light into your womb space by removing your hands from the mudra and putting your hands flat onto the area.

~ You can place this energy anywhere you like, such as onto a vision board, or onto a sick pet.

~ You could even offer it to Lady Hope to use wherever it's needed in the world.

This is a really lovely exercise that you can use each day with minimal effort. It'll remind you of your magnificent capabilities when utilizing your feminine superpowers.

The Annunciating Duo

Lady Hope belongs to the fourth white ray of the angelic kingdom and her masculine counterpart is Archangel Gabriel. Archangel Gabriel is the most feminine of all of the Archangels and is sometimes even depicted as being female by many artists. The pure white light that these twin rays embody is very sweet and innocent, making this duo the perfect candidates to guide and protect children, including those raising them. Archangel Gabriel is their protector and teacher, while Lady Hope helps us adults to be more like them – curious and open-hearted!

Together, these angels govern the legions of the Angels of Purity. These highly evolved angels who work under this Divine ray operate around the clock, spreading their crystal-clear diamond light into the hearts of those who've asked for forgiveness or clarity.

Their etheric retreat portal is at Mount Shasta, USA. However, you can travel there in your mind, rather than in physical form, and it's just as powerful. You can ask Archangel Gabriel or Lady Hope to take you to their portal when you sleep.

Archangel Gabriel

Archangel Gabriel, otherwise known as 'God is my strength', is such an amazing gentle, loving angel. His presence is like a sweet balm for your spirit. He's the ultimate messenger angel, announcing good news in myths and lore since time immemorial. In the Judgement Tarot card, Archangel Gabriel blows his lily horn, capturing your attention as he readies himself to make a grand announcement. His call comes so loudly that it even wakes the dead from their coffins, resembling how his words reverberate through your soul, probing you to assess your life. When we ignore making necessary changes in life, we can be given a wake-up call such as an illness that forces us to reflect and change. Archangel Gabriel is the angel who whispers suggestions and gentle advice to you along the way. If you heed his advice, harsh circumstances can be avoided.

Archangel Gabriel can help you with any form of communication large or small, from penning a book to getting your point across to another person in a peaceful manner. Whatever you need to say, just invite him to stand by your side and ask him to pour pure thoughts into your aura.

Archangel Gabriel also assists with fertility, pregnancy, childbirth, rearing children and healing your inner child wounds. He supports parents, midwives, school teachers and anyone who works with children. He helps to restore you to the innocence and purity of the inner child.

Working with Lady Hope

Lady Hope has unique associations that can further enhance a connection with her. If you like, you can set up an altar to infuse your intentions with her vibrations of hope. I suggest using or wearing items in the colour black for manifesting (the womb/cosmic void) or orange for enthusiasm and creativity. I recommend burning essential oils such as rose, geranium or spikenard.

Lady Hope's Gemstones

The following crystals have the healing vibrations that will resonate when working with Lady Hope:

- Herkimer diamond
- orange calcite
- jasper
- citrine
- spirit quartz

The crystals listed are perfect to help you to achieve all of your wishes. Holding or wearing them will attune you to the high-vibrational energy of Lady Hope.

Once you've gathered your items, try this next invocation so that you can experience her energy first hand:

INVOCATION: CALLING IN LADY HOPE

Use this short invocation to call in the presence of Lady Hope any time you need an injection of hope or optimism. It can be helpful to use this ritual daily when you're working towards manifesting a goal.

You will need:

~ a white candle

~ matches

~ a pen and a piece of paper

When you perform this ritual, find a quiet place where you can relax in peace. Then take a few deep breaths to calm and centre yourself, and begin:

~ Raise your vibration by thinking of a time when you felt lucky or blessed.

~ Invoke Lady Hope by whispering her name three times.

~ With your hands in the prayer position, say, 'Lady Hope, Lady Hope, Lady Hope.'

~ Light a candle in her honour.

~ State: 'Wish of the Goddess, hold me tight, forever sealed in your cloak of light. I ask you to infuse me with your hopeful glow as it is in heaven as it is below.'

~ Imagine or feel Lady Hope placing a sparkly white cloak over your shoulders.

~ She pulls the hood over your head and fastens it with a gold brooch in the shape of the fleur-de-lis.

~ Take a few minutes to bask in her delightful energy.

~ Feel this Archeia's joy and hope spread out into your aura.

~ Notice a tingling in your Sacral chakra.

~ An orange glow begins to emerge and expand into a ball, which pulsates like a radiant orange sun.

~ Allow it to move around your body.

~ Take it down through your hips, legs and feet.

~ Then take it up through your belly, chest and throat.

~ See it spread down each arm, up into your head.

~ Finally, visualize it resting back where it began, in the Sacral chakra.

~ Place your hands on your belly to seal the energy into your Sacral chakra.

~ When you're ready, close your Sacral chakra down by imagining that orange light getting smaller and dimmer until it resembles a small flame.

~ Remember to give thanks.

~ Take some notes of your experience to help you to recognize the energetic differences between the Archeiai.

~ Ground your energy by stamping your feet for a few seconds.

~ Go about your day fuelled with energy and optimism.

Lady Hope has a wonderful pick-me-up energy. Continue to use this invocation regularly to keep your arms and mind open to receiving her many blessings. When you embody her energy, you'll also find that you have the physical energy to see projects through to the end.

This next powerful mini ritual and visualization will allow you to enter the cosmic womb of the universe. In this space, all potential outcomes exist. Here, you can retrieve the energetic blueprint of your wishes, with the ritual seeding your intention from mass to matter. We'll be journeying with Lady Hope and the power animal totem of the raven. Negative superstitions surrounding ravens are once again an attempt to reinforce patriarchy. Why? Because ravens represent the feminine. These holy birds can accompany you into the womb of the Great Mother Goddess, helping you to achieve your heart's desire. Being around these magical creatures will heighten your intuition and your sense of claircognizance. Being linked to the powers of Air, they carry your prayers on their wings.

ENTERING THE COSMIC VOID

For your ritual journey, we'll be working with the magical powers of Lady Hope and the raven totem.

You will need:

~ an intention – what do you wish to manifest?

~ a pen and a piece of paper

~ a black candle

~ matches

~ spikenard or lavender essential oil

~ trance-inducing music such as shamanic drumming, Krishna Das, Sadhguru, or Deva Premal (all of which can be found on YouTube)

~ Herkimer diamond crystal (optional)

~ a dried herb bundle for burning

~ salt for ritual bathing such as a handful of sea salt, Himalayan salt or Epsom salts

Before your ritual journey, prepare your body by bathing in salt and clear your working space by burning herbs.

Ensure you find somewhere peaceful and quiet, then begin:

~ Invoke the presence of Lady Hope by placing your hands in the prayer posture and calling her name three times.

~ Say, 'Lady Hope, Lady Hope, Lady Hope.'

~ Watch her place angelic protection over you.

~ See yourself wearing her shimmering white cloak to raise and protect your energy.

~ Ask Lady Hope to travel with you for the entire journey.

~ Say, 'Lady Hope, thank you for placing your angelic protection over me. Please hold my hand and guide me every step of the way. Thank you, Angels of Purity, for holding my body in sacred space while I travel on this journey.'

~ Write your intention on a piece of paper and place it on the floor in front of you.

~ Light the black candle, dedicating it to the raven, stating: 'If it is for the good of all, including myself, then, Raven dark, Raven night, Raven bring me your magical sight. Eyes that see magic, wings that travel realms, carry my intention of [add your wish] from where the invisible dwells. Cosmic womb, please bless what I am about to birth, to witness here on Planet Earth.'

~ Place one drop of spikenard or lavender essential oil on the sole of each foot to protect you when walking through worlds.

~ Lie down in a warm, comfortable place.

~ Place the crystal over your Sacral chakra, just underneath the belly button.

~ Closing your eyes, listen to the music for at least 15 to 20 minutes.

~ Keeping your attention on your sacral area, imagine that you're breathing in through the front of this chakra (in front of you) and breathing out through the back of it (behind you).

~ Imagine or feel Lady Hope now bringing through the medicine of the raven power animal.

~ You take a moment to acknowledge this magnificent black bird by looking into his eyes and asking for help with your wish.

~ The raven taps his beak three times onto the wall, where a solid black crystal door appears.

~ As the door opens, you feel a gentle cool breeze on your face.

~ Behind the door lies a night sky of twinkling stars.

~ You climb on raven's back, holding onto his feathers, which shimmer with hues of bright blues and silver.

~ You take off into the night sky, Lady Hope by your side and with your written intention in the raven's beak.

~ You stop in front of a star and the raven places your intention directly onto it.

~ Other stars nearby draw closer, forming a unique constellation that visually represents your wish.

~ This pattern is the energetic blueprint of your wish.

~ Stand before the constellation, slowly absorbing its powerful cosmic energies into your own aura, where these frequencies will be housed until the perfect time to birth.

~ These hopes will manifest as wisdom, opportunity and divinely guided ideas.

~ When you're ready, travel back into the room.

~ Safely close the crystal door behind you.

~ Come back to the here and now.

~ Wiggle your fingers and toes and take a big stretch.

~   Give thanks to the raven and Lady Hope.

~   Smile in the knowledge that your wish is now written in the stars.

~   To ground your energy completely, have a bite to eat.

You can call upon the medicine of the raven any time you wish to enter other dimensions to retrieve their energetic blueprint or seed. This method is one of the most powerful ways to set your intentions into the universe. After all, the cosmic womb is the place where all things are originally birthed. Lady Hope will ensure that you only ever call things in from a high place of integrity, for the good of all.

Have you ever heard of the term cosmic egg? Ancient yogis believe that the very universe is shaped as an egg. Using an egg-shaped crystal to manifest rather than a regular tumble stone can give your wish that extra edge. This is partly down to the influence that the shape has on our subconscious mind. In symbology, the egg represents the womb, fertility, abundance and new beginnings.

MANIFESTING WITH A CRYSTAL EGG

Purchase an egg-shaped crystal of any size that has properties that closely align with the nature of your wish. For example:

~   black for protection

~   blue for communication

~   clear for clarity

~   green for healing

~   orange for inspiration

~   pink for love

~   purple for spirituality

~   red for energy

~   white for angels

~   yellow for happiness

Making a magical mojo pouch

You're probably familiar with the saying 'I've lost my mojo' when someone's lost their desire for something. Or the phrase 'I've got my mojo back' when someone's feeling inspired once again. The word 'mojo' refers to life force or energy.

Placing your crystal egg into a mojo bag feeds it with energy, keeping your wish nurtured.

These types of amulets have their roots in hoodoo folk magic. I've had spectacular results with mojo bags. It's a must-try magical tool! This ritual is best performed during a new moon.

You will need:

~   your chosen crystal egg cleansed with salt or herb smoke

~   a piece of black material representing the womb that's big enough to store your egg

~   8 dried cloves

~   8 drops of orange essential oil

~   a needle and cotton

~   a small piece of paper and a pen

~   an orange, yellow or gold candle

~   a small piece of string to tie the pouch

~   matches

Before you start, clear your space by carrying a bundle of burning herbs anticlockwise around the room three times, then open a window and imagine the smoke carrying out any negative energy.

~ Light the candle.

~ Call in Lady Hope by saying, 'Lady Hope, Lady Hope, Lady Hope, I call upon your sacred Divine feminine energy now to protect and bless both me and my space with your holy presence. Thank you.'

~ Write on the piece of paper: Thank you for [add your wish].

~ Thinking of your wish manifest, fold the material in half and stitch the two sides together.

~ Holding the egg in your right hand, program it by requesting how you'd like it to help you.

~ Place the egg into the pouch along with the 8 cloves.

~ Add the 8 drops of oil to the bag.

~ Place your piece of paper with your written wish into the bag.

~ Tie the final opening with string.

~ Activate the bag by placing it at your Third Eye chakra on your forehead.

~ Once again, visualize how happy you'll feel once your bag has worked its magic.

~ Blow onto the bag, breathing it to life.

~ Give thanks to Lady Hope, the crystal and your protectors.

~ Each day, 'feed the bag' by again placing it at the Third Eye chakra and thinking of your wish until it's fulfilled – remember, everything occurs in Divine timing.

~ When the magic has worked, scatter the contents of the pouch on the ground.

~ Ethically dispose of the pouch and cleanse the crystal (with smoke or salt) to reset it to a neutral point, ready to be reprogrammed again with another manifestation.

Ancient magical rituals such as this are very effective in assisting you in harnessing life-force energies. They serve as a focal point and a reminder of where you're placing your attention. May all of your wishes be granted.

We're truly blessed to have Lady Hope and her inspiring team of angels to watch over us and remind us of our purpose on Earth: to cocreate a life filled with fun, joy and love. Please remember to ask her to help you in the birthing of any project. She's only too happy to help.

CHAPTER 9

Lady Mary
Queen of Angels

Archeia Mary, the 'Queen of Angels', is a very high-dimensional light being. She's so spiritually immaculate that only those with the purest of intentions have the ability to see her physically.

Her name has several very interesting root meanings and translations that each represent the complexity of her core essence and how interwoven she actually is with humanity, despite so little being known about her directly. Lady Mary can be traced to the derivations of 'Myrrh', 'Mistress of the Sea', 'Star of the Sea' (Stella Maris) and 'Beloved of Amun'.

Archeia Mary has guided humanity eternally. She's the exemplar of what it truly means to be of service. She works with Archangel Raphael to teach humanity how to be of service, how to heal their life and how to become a pure vessel able to channel the highest quality of light.

Lady Mary's Appearance

Lady Mary is more easily felt than seen. In her energetic light body, she emanates from the Diamond Heart of Source in all shades of glistening greens and shimmering blues. If you perceive her in a physical form, she may appear wearing a white dress cloaked with her iconic blue shawl of light. Every time I've seen her, her head has always been covered, loosely shrouded with her blue shawl. She wears a golden Egyptian ankh around her neck. Her eyes are hypnotic, sparkling like precious green jewels. She looks at you like a mother looks at her newborn baby for the first time: love at first sight.

Lady Mary's Energy

Lady Mary has a beautiful, loving energy. To be in her presence is an absolute honour. I feel as though I want to take a bow of respect and sometimes I do. Not out worship or idolizing her but rather as a mark of the deeply heartfelt gratitude that arises from receiving her gifts.

She's the archetypal mother who adores all of her children. She's soft and youthful in her demeanour.

She can help you with:

- healing yourself and others
- being of service to the Divine
- hearing your prayers
- honouring the divinity within you
- guidance during motherhood
- accessing your sacred feminine qualities
- channelling high-vibrational healing energy
- promoting generosity

- developing virtues

- following your own star

- discovering your galactic past lives or soul origin

Lady Mary's Calling Cards

Listed below are Archeia Mary's bespoke calling cards which may appear when she's near:

- Her soul number vibration is 12. You may see it in various repetitious forms such 1212. A nice wholesome number, we have 12 planets, astrological months, Archangelic temples, chakras and DNA strands. The number 12 contains the essence of everything having a place that dances in harmony with all of creation.

- Lady Mary's animals are white doves, signifying purity, and blue butterflies, signifying transformation and healing the watery feminine. If you work with Lady Mary, it's likely that you'll see these animals in the following days as a little confirmation from her that she's there with you.

- You may feel extreme peace wash over you when she's around. You'll feel very loved and cared for. As she stirs your heart centre, you'll automatically extend these loving feelings to those around you. You'll perceive them both in their innocence and their divinity.

- After you've been in her presence, you'll feel spiritually clean and pure, like you've been reborn.

- Her flowers are the assumption lily and blue roses (love at first sight).

Angel of Service

All angels are in service to the Divine. This means that they devote their existence to the one greater unity, consciousness. Angels work for the good of others. They're above personal desire and it's their choice to dedicate their light to bringing about the highest good for all beings.

Archeia Mary guides those who are ready to rise into their immaculate heart, to surpass all selfish needs and desires, and to be of service to the Creator. Lady Mary reiterates that to be in service doesn't mean that you have to be chastised, give away all of your possessions or become a nun.

To be in service means to honour the God/dess within you. She says that people give away their power by worshipping a force outside of them. In truth, the Goddess flows through every inch of your being. So, to live a life in service is to surrender to your personal truth by following your higher self-guidance.

Mother Mary, mother of Jesus, is sometimes depicted with 12 stars above her head. This is because she followed the guidance from Archangel Mary – to follow her star and successfully reconnect her 12-strand DNA.

If you feel like you could be a better person, if you want to stop judging or become kinder, call upon Archeia Mary. She'll plant a star in your aura to be your guiding light. It'll remind you that you always have a choice and there's always another way. If you're aligned with your soul, then you're aligned with the Creator. If you're acting upon the wishes of your soul, you become the Divine embodiment.

Lady Mary says that you're perfect in every way. Your soul already contains all of the holy virtues such as generosity and compassion. It's simply a case of reconnecting to that sacred place within you. Your responses will always be in accordance with the Divine once you've mastered living from the heart. She'll help you to commit to serving your higher self-guidance or to anything that'll bring about a more harmonious lifestyle.

Angel of Mothers

Sweet Lady Mary bestows extra-special blessings towards mothers and their children. She offers her assistance in many ways, including healing relationships with your own children and your parents.

Archangel Mary was the personal advisor of Mary. Although Christianity implies that Mary was a Jew, probably from Nazareth, the birthplace of Jesus, she was in fact from Egypt. Within the cult of Isis, Mary was a very high initiate. So much so that on attainment of her virginal state, where she reclaimed her sovereignty, she was elected by the Council of Light to be in further service by rearing and moulding a master in the making: Jesus.

As instructed by Archeia Mary, she travelled to Jerusalem, where she met her husband, St Joseph – the embodiment of St Germain. Together, these spiritual Masters were the perfect candidates to prepare Jesus as the Christ bearer of the Piscean Age. Mother Mary demonstrated complete devotion to her son. She knew of His destiny before He was even conceived. What an extraordinarily difficult task that must have been for her: to know she'd lose her beloved son at the age of just 33.

Archeia Mary continued to guide Mother Mary throughout her life, assigned to her like a guardian angel. She settled her mind in moments of worry and held her in compassion during her bereavement. You can call upon the blessings of Archeia Mary to hold and protect your children. Whether they're battling an illness or are simply having a sleepover at a friend's house, she'll shield them under her wings and even perform a miracle if it's of the highest will of God.

When my five-year-old daughter endured a 10-hour operation to save her arm and required an artery transplant after a horrific injury, my faith was tested to the max. Far from being composed, I was devastated and overcome with fear. Especially when everything that could have gone wrong in her surgery did so. During this crisis, my fear urged me to pray to Archangel Mary and every Master and angel that I knew of for reassurance of her recovery.

But I needn't have done so. Archangel Mary's protection would have sufficed, but because I was overcome with fear, my vibration became too low for me to hear her whispers of comfort. The only angel who could reach me was Archangel Michael. He simply said, 'The worst is now behind you,' and I knew with all my heart that his words were the complete truth.

Archangel Mary can also help you with any wounds that you have from your childhood, including mother and father wounding (traumatic experiences involving those who raised you). The cause of mother or father wounds might be the death of a parent or being looked after by a caregiver who was emotionally unavailable to you when you were a child.

The wounding can be so deep that it unconsciously affects your relationships with men or women who you encounter throughout your life. They could well be the seeds that still sprout into negative patterns today. So many of my clients have come to realize during a reading that the reason behind why they can't manifest their dreams is down to a limited programming that they've inherited from a parent. The absence of a parent has created a huge lack of self-worth, thought to be the collective consciousness, which seems obvious. Since the reign of patriarchy, we've been left motherless.

Here's a prayer that Archeia Mary, Queen of the Angels, taught me. It can be used to manifest a blessing for a child or yourself:

Dear Mary, I call upon your light to enfold me in a compassionate embrace. Thank you for shielding [me/child/parent] from harshness and harm. By the power of grace, by the power of love, Mary of the Sea, our guiding star to love.

Angel Encounter

I was introduced to Archeia Mary fairly late in comparison to the other Archangels, whom I've known since I was a little girl. The first time I met her was simple to say the least and without any elaborate ceremony. She simply popped in to visit me one night. It would have been 2005 because I was in Somerset, where I only lived for a short time. I'd been contemplating the possible meaning of a strange coincidence and I suppose I was looking for answers.

You see, I'd recently discovered that over 60 years ago, my nan had given birth to a stillborn son, Michael. During a complicated labour, the umbilical cord had wrapped itself around his neck, sadly taking his life. What struck me about the story was the fact that my uncle Michael was born on 11 November (11.11) – the same date that I'd given birth to my daughter Leah. Similarly, during my labour, the umbilical cord had become entangled around her neck. I'd prayed for a miracle and she'd freed herself seconds before I was about to be rushed for an emergency caesarean section.

Adding to the whirring of my wild thoughts was the astonishing fact that uncannily, both babies were also born at the *exact* same time! You know where I'm going with this?

So, there I was, trying to get to sleep this particular night with all of these mysterious occurrences running through my brain; I was trying to figure out what it might mean when Archeia Mary appeared beside my bed. I had no idea who she was and nor did I get time to ask, as she simply said, 'Write Michael backwards,' then disappeared.

Excited, I grabbed a pen. A wave of goose bumps broke out all over my body as I wrote LAEHCIM (besides the letter C, an anagram of 'I'm Leah'). Was this angel confirming my speculations? Why had she prompted me to write down this name? Was Leah the incarnation of Michael? I wondered in awe.

What's interesting to me is that whenever I write Michael and Raphael, my instinct is always to spell them wrong. I always type: Micheal and Rapheal. This way of spelling seems perfect to me because they both end with 'heal'. Of course, the 'el' at the end of some angel names denotes their status as Divine beings. *El* or *Elohim* is Hebrew for God.

I got to know Archeia Mary very well after this initial brief encounter and she always pops in when it's child-related. In another encounter I'd been to visit a sick relative in hospital. On the way back to the car park I searched my bag for the parking ticket. My two daughters were with me and I was conscious of crossing the road and getting them safely into the car. Relieved to sit down, I slumped myself into the driver's seat, and then the girls began bickering in the back. 'Why are you putting a seat belt on no one?' Leah snorted to Lexi, who was indeed unnecessarily plugging in the middle seat belt.

Brows raised, she said, 'I'm putting it on Lucy!' Even though I'm clairvoyant, I'd been too distracted in the hustle and bustle to notice that a little girl had left the hospital with us in spirit. Lucy was happy as Larry, chatting away to Lexi like a friend.

The poor little soul hadn't realized she'd passed. I immediately called in my guardian angel and asked, 'Who shall I call in?' I agreed whole-heartedly when she said, 'Lady Mary.'

I whispered her name three times and Lady Mary swooped in immediately. Already aware of the situation, she'd also brought in Lucy's grandma, a lady she'd known very closely in Lucy's short life. They embraced each other tightly and away they all went. It was an incredibly emotional experience. I'm glad that Lucy latched onto us that day. She received a healing from Lady Mary and now she's where she's supposed to be.

Angel of Healers

Lady Mary is the Angel of Healers. If you're a healer, then I definitely recommend that you use my exercise to attune yourself to her energy. Even if you've had energy healing attunements before, the more highly evolved you become, the more light you can contain. Lady Mary will take your skills to the next level.

For example, when I was giving energy healing sessions, I'd instinctively know where my client was depleted and what symptoms they were suffering from, but it was Lady Mary or Archangel Raphael who'd explain to me what thoughts and unresolved trauma had actually manifested the symptoms in the first place. Getting to the heart of the matter ensured that the symptoms disappeared forever.

If you want to train as a professional healer, ask Lady Mary to guide you to the perfect teacher. Likewise, if you or a loved one require a good healthcare practitioner or therapist, just ask Lady Mary. She'll source them and draw your attention to them like a magnet. Lady Mary says that we're all capable of healing.

The Emerald Duo

Lady Mary is the twin ray Divine counterpart to Archangel Raphael. They work on the fifth angelic ray - the emerald ray of healing, truth and science. Together, they oversee the legions of the angels of healing, who tend to the emerald flame and distribute it across the world. They overlight hospitals, singing harmonics to the 963 Hz solfeggio frequency.

This frequency activates and heals the Third Eye chakra. Focusing on positive thoughts is essential to ensure the best chance of a recovery taking place. The placebo effect proves that the power of your own mind can heal you. Interestingly, it's estimated that approximately a third of prescription drugs and surgeries are successful through the placebo effect. Those who expect a treatment to work have a much higher chance of recovery, whereas those who expect failure are the most likely candidates to endure an unsuccessful prescribed medicine or failed medical procedure.

These powerful healing frequencies encourage you to perceive yourself in perfect health and will remind you to be mindful of making good healthcare choices. If you require a more optimistic outlook on your health, you can call upon Archangel Raphael to clear your Third Eye chakra. He'll pull away the veils that cloud the perfect vision of your health.

If you're sick, you can ask Archangel Raphael and Lady Mary to place an emerald-green healing blanket over you while you sleep. You'll wake feeling more optimistic and with improved health. Their etheric healing temple is Fatima, Portugal. However, Mother Mary has her own portal, which is in Lourdes, France.

Archangel Raphael

Archangel Raphael, 'whom God heals', is renowned as the heavenly physician and through the Third Eye chakra he helps us to manifest perfect health using our imagination. He's a gentle angel who's most often silent. He's an avid teacher through the means of exploration. Archangel Raphael's biggest hope for you is that you free your mind from what you've 'learned' so that you can become an empty vessel, open to receiving an authentic, unadulterated wisdom of science and technology.

Archangel Raphael has acted as the silent bystander of all of the great minds and inventors, gently stimulating their minds to wonderment. We live in exciting times, where after thousands of years science is marrying with the spiritual knowledge of what the mystics have known since time immemorial. Similarly, the marrying of Divine feminine and masculine principles will bring us the whole truth of who we really are, opening us up to what we're capable of.

Working with Lady Mary

Many people have unknowingly experienced the energies of Archeia Mary by praying to Mother Mary. She's such a powerful angel to call in that she touches your heart on such a deep level. When working with Archeia Mary, I may wear white or blue clothes, burn white candles and burn rose essential oil. These items will align you with her vibration perfectly. I always like to offer her a bunch of roses as a symbol of my gratitude (although that's a personal preference, of course).

Lady Mary's Gemstones

The following crystals have the healing properties that resonate with the energy of Lady Mary:

- aquamarine

- emerald

- malachite

- blue lace agate

- snowy quartz

- Lemurian clear quartz

- sapphires

These beautiful gemstones are very pure in healing energy. They'll uplift your emotional body (aura) and reawaken the sleeping feminine wisdom within you. From your clear perspective you'll access unlimited blessings. Everything that you need to know in regard to healing yourself and others will be revealed to you. Wear or hold any of these precious gemstones when you're calling in a blessing from Lady Mary.

 ## INVOCATION: CALLING IN LADY MARY

This invocation will allow you to experience the lovely energy of Archeia Mary. Of course, you can simply state her name three times out loud, but I think it shows respect and commitment on your behalf if you put in some extra effort from time to time. It's nice to have gratitude for your angelic friends.

If you're setting up an altar as a small offering, create this first with the suggested items earlier (see Working with Lady Mary) and then call her in.

You will need:

~ a blue candle

~ an oil burner with 4 drops of rose essential oil

~ a glass of water

Begin by lighting the burner and adding the oil to the water, then light your candle:

~ With your hands in a prayer posture, say, 'Beloved Archeia Mary, I invite you to stand by my side. I wish to know you and become the embodiment of your loving ways. I am Lady Mary, I am the immaculate heart, I am blessed by Mary, Queen of the Angels. Amen.'

~ Place your hands over the glass of water and sing, 'Mare-Ray, Mare-Ray, Mare-Ray.'

~ Now, close your eyes and place your hands gently on your lap.

~ Imagine or feel her beautiful presence swooping in.

~ She's smiling with joy to see you.

~ Lady Mary places an etheric sapphire chalice into your Heart chakra.

~ In your inner vision, dive into the waters of your own soul.

~ Explore this new territory.

~ Trust any messages or visions that come to mind.

~ When you feel ready, open your eyes and wiggle your fingers and toes.

~ Write about your experience.

~ Drink the water, which is now blessed holy water.

~ Give thanks to Lady Mary and look out for her confirmation signs.

Lady Mary will help you to open your immaculate heart. This is your own angel heart, which is pure and loves unconditionally. Call in Lady Mary to clear your emotions and to help you to perceive the angel within each person.

We each have the ability to tap in to the ever-giving, ever-flowing rivers of healing energy. You can receive an attunement from a master energy healer, or you can receive them from the angels themselves. I've experienced both, yet the most profound channels that were awakened within me were from Archangel Raphael and Archeia Mary.

An attunement is simply the fine-tuning of your energy bodies and chakras to enable them to become a channelling vessel. An initiation is a starting point from which to initiate or begin. Not all of us want to become professional healers, yet it's still a nice practice to calibrate your energy centres in order to receive unlimited amounts of high-quality light. You can give this energy to others when needed, like a child or a pet, or use it simply to store within yourself.

CHANNELLING ANGELIC HEALING ENERGY

You'll need to take a ritual bath for this exercise. I recommend a handful of sea salt and a few sprigs of rosemary. Create a sacred space with candles and incense. Use whatever methods you like to create a spiritual atmosphere. You're best seated in an upright position for this exercise:

~ Call in Archeia Mary, Archangel Raphael and the Angels of the Emerald Ray.

~ With your hands in the prayer posture, say, 'Beloved Mary, Queen of the Angels, I call upon your light and love. Beloved Raphael, physician of heaven, I call upon your light and love. Beloved angels of healing, keepers of the emerald ray, I call upon your light and love. Thank you for blessing me with your Divine presence.'

~ The room is now flooded with happy angels who continue to flock in, raising the vibration of your sacred space.

~ Lady Mary and Archangel Raphael look deeply into your eyes as you explain that you'd like to align your energy with their healing light.

~ Express how you'd be of service to others by blessing them with healing energy once you've healed yourself.

~ Place your palms facing upwards and feel a gentle heat beginning to build in your palms.

~ Archangel Raphael places a gold-and-green ball of light into your cupped hands.

~ Feel the energy ball becoming warmer and slightly heavier while taking very slow, deep breaths in through your nose and out through your mouth.

~ When your hands are sufficiently full of energy, they'll begin to tingle, indicating that you've gathered enough energy.

~ Place both hands, palms flat, gently on the crown of your head for two to three minutes.

~ Gently remove your hands.

~ In a downwards motion, sweep your hands over your face (in the aura) without physically touching your skin.

~ Continue by smoothing the healing energy down over your shoulders.

~ Slowly smooth the energy out over your entire body, extending out to everywhere you can reach, including under the soles of your feet.

~ You'll feel a buzzing sensation between the skin of your body and your palms.

~ Now, focus your attention on an abundant reservoir of cosmic healing light, which the healing angels are holding over your Crown chakra.

~ Imagine a ray of this light touching the top of your head and travelling down, passing through the Third Eye and Throat chakras, and into the Heart chakra.

~ This energy blesses your Heart chakra with an abundance of healing energy.

~ Now, visualize two glistening green energy pathways sprouting from your Heart chakra, one on either side.

~ The two channels travel into each of your shoulders and down each arm, one either side, coming to rest in the palm of each hand.

~ Place your palms together in prayer position.

~ Chant the sound 'ahhh' seven times to activate your Palm chakras.

~ Pull your hands apart and visualize or feel the energy travelling from the reservoir, through your upper chakras and down into the palms, gently bursting out of your hands like a fountain.

~ Physically place your hands on your body wherever you feel you could benefit from the healing energy the most.

~ When you're ready, visualize the angels disconnecting you from the reservoir of light that was above your head and carrying it off into the distance.

~ Give thanks to Lady Mary and Archangel Raphael.

~ Take as much time as you need before you ground your energy by stamping your feet on the ground or having a herbal tea and a light snack.

~ If possible, only eat fruit, vegetables and rice for the next 24 to 48 hours to integrate the high energy for as long as you can.

After you've initiated the use of your energy channels, you'll be able to channel the purest high-vibrational angelic energy to heal yourself.

I recommend that you practise using this energy for yourself first before trying it on others, should you feel compelled to do so. Here's a step-by-step process that you can use to offer healing to others:

PERFORMING AN ENERGY HEALING SESSION

The aforementioned initiation process only needs to be performed once during a healing session, so once you've done it the first time, you can go straight into the next part.

You will need:

~ a grounding stone such as black tourmaline or smoky quartz.

~ a bundle of aura-cleansing herbs

~ a lighter

~ a fireproof tray to catch any hot herbs that drop out

~ relaxing Zen or spa music (there are plenty of free resources on YouTube)

Before the person arrives for the healing, clear your aura and space with dried herb smoke and put your psychic protection in place.

~ Call in Archeia Mary, Archangel Raphael and the healing angels of the emerald ray.

~ Invite your client to sit or lie down and ask them to close their eyes – soft music may help them to relax during the session.

~ Clear their aura by gently wafting the dried herb smoke around the outside of their body (be mindful of hot herbs potentially dropping on them by using a dish to catch anything that might fall).

~ Place your hands on your client's shoulders, either physically or in their aura.

~ Ask the healing angels to place the green-and-gold reservoir ball of healing light above your head.

~ With your spine straight, begin to breathe deeply, in through the nose and out through the mouth.

~ As the energy starts to build in intensity, feel it begin to penetrate your Crown chakra (the top of your head may tingle or feel very hot).

~ With each in breath, begin to draw the energy down into your Heart chakra and out of your hands.

~ Feel your hands beginning to tingle as they each project a ray of healing emerald light.

~ Direct the energy by saying, 'For the highest good of all, energy, go where you are needed.'

~ At some point you'll feel the energy switch off, indicating it's time to finish.

~ Disconnect your Crown chakra from the healing energy.

~ Close your Palm chakras by visualizing them sealing up.

~ Give thanks to the angels.

~ Ensure that the receiver is fully grounded by holding their feet for a few minutes and sitting them up slowly.

~ Check whether or not they feel light-headed or spaced out, or if they feel fine now.

~ If further grounding is required, offering them a drink or a dark crystal to hold for 5–10 minutes will help with this.

~ Advise them to relax for the rest of the day if possible.

~ Take a bath or shower to clear your own energy.

Offering healing to others is a very rewarding practice. You'll develop your psychic awareness and deepen your bond with the angels by doing so. However, if you're not feeling 100 per cent yourself, then reserve the healing for you personally until you're feeling strong. Energy is contagious and by channelling it, you imprint your personal energy onto it to some degree.

You shouldn't get tired or drained from giving energy healing. In fact, it's quite the opposite. You should be receiving some of the energy yourself because you're not spending your own energy. It's a gift from the universe. If you find you are tired, then ensure you use adequate psychic protection. Read the chapter on Lady Faith for more assistance with this.

Star of the Sea

Archeia Mary can help you to remain true to your higher vision, your soul's greatest destiny, by implanting a high-vibrational star vortex within your aura. This star can be thought of as a compass. So long as you tune in to it for a few minutes each day, this star will give you a nudge if you begin to veer off course. How amazing would that be, to have your own personal star that reminds you to stay on course!

I've used this star to complete this book. I've had to create a lot of new habits and be very disciplined in order to write it. I have a very busy lifestyle – husband, kids, visits to the gym and my own business to run – so without Lady Mary's star I'd have slipped into the temptation of wasting time. Whether it be coffee afternoons with friends or scrolling too long on Facebook, the star has reigned me in before I've lost my opportunity to write. Lady Mary's star also reminds you how much your dreams will be worth it once they manifest. That's certainly a good way of enhancing your motivation.

IMPLANTING LADY MARY'S GUIDING STAR

This star is merely a tool that will assist you in remaining committed to your higher-self wisdom and your destiny. You can ask Lady Mary to dissolve the star if for any reason you wish to remove it.

All you'll need for this exercise is a white candle and some matches. I always offer a gift of gratitude to all beings who help me, even if it's by simply lighting a candle. It's a good idea to have a ritual bath prior to embarking on this exercise. Try a handful of ground sea salt, a few drops of rose essential oil and a handful of rose petals. When you're prepared, make sure you find somewhere quiet where you can relax undisturbed.

~   Dedicate your candle by lighting it and saying, 'Lady Mary, I light this candle in your name.'

~   With your hands in the prayer posture, call in Archeia Mary by saying, 'Queen of Angels, Queen of the Sea, Queen of the Stars, Queen of Me. Lady Mary, angel sweet and true, cover me in your cloak of blue.'

~ Imagine Lady Mary as an incredibly beautiful angel stood in front of you now.

~ Her light emerald-green aura expands around her like gentle waves of the ocean.

~ Your Third Eye chakra begins to tingle across your forehead as it draws Lady Mary's green watery aura towards it.

~ Take a deep breath in through your nose and out through your mouth.

~ Now, allow her light to penetrate the Third Eye chakra, slowly filling your entire body with her glowing light.

~ This light seals each cell in your body with the consciousness of the immaculate heart – pure and spotlessly clean.

~ When your insides are brimming with light, allow the light to radiate out into your aura, shining brightly and lighting your face.

~ You notice a golden crown of light on Lady Mary's head, with 13 golden stars (including an extra one for you) twinkling upon it.

~ Lady Mary takes one of the stars and holds it over your Heart chakra.

~ Think about what you truly want in your life.

~ Your heart's desires are infused with the star and are sealed up safely inside it.

~ Lady Mary raises the star and places it inside your aura, about 20 centimetres (8 inches) out, just above your forehead.

~ Place your hands on the star together with Lady Mary.

~ Declare three times, 'I will follow the star of my highest truth.'

~ Place your hands into the prayer position just over your Heart chakra while Lady Mary seals your star into your aura.

~ Thank Lady Mary with all of your heart.

Use this exercise any time you embark upon a new project to keep you in alignment with your goals. If you feel as though you're on the wrong path, or are unsure of what your path entails, then implant the star with the intention of guiding you to your highest destiny, or simply to happiness.

Tips for Using Your Star

My advice would be to ask Lady Mary how to utilize this star yourself. This is a lesson in trusting your own Divine wisdom. However, here are three tips to get you started:

1. Daily Intention-Setting

Each morning when I wake, I set intentions into my guiding star. I think of three things that I intend to achieve that day. For example, I might decide that I want to:

- go to the gym (something for me)

- write my full moon newsletter (something for work)

- make healthy food and drink choices (something for my temple)

I then visualize my golden star lighting up and I program it by thinking or saying, 'Today, I've been to the gym. I've finished writing my newsletter. I've eaten clean foods all day and I've only drunk water. I feel fantastic that I've achieved these amazing things for myself.'

Notice how I've affirmed my vision in the past tense? I've set my destiny before it's even happened.

Have a big stretch and go about your day. Of course, you may need to make a plan or schedule adequate time into your diary by literally giving yourself an appointment time to get the ball rolling.

Setting dates with yourself will ensure that you commit to taking the necessary action.

If you feel tempted throughout the day to go off course, your light will trigger you into remembering your goals. For example, if you get tempted by a delicious chocolate cake or pulled onto social media with a ping from the phone, your star will attempt to recover the situation by grabbing your attention. You could experience a hot sensation or tingling of the forehead. You might see flashing twinkly lights. Or you may see your star light up clairvoyantly. Or it may even question you directly and ask, 'How does this serve you?'

2. Be in the Right Place at the Right Time

In the same vein as the aforementioned exercise, you can also program your star to ensure that you're in the right place at the right time. We've all been in those situations where we've ended up somewhere totally random that's led us to uncover something amazing.

When a venue I used to hire closed down I set my star to help me to find the perfect new venue for my angel communication course. I was very specific and asked for a beautiful light room with windows all the way around it – like a conservatory – and with doors that opened up into gardens.

Now at the time, a venue of this description was unheard of near me, but that was exactly what I wanted, so that's the intention that I put into my star. A few days later my children broke up from school for half term. My youngest had been given a free local magazine called *What's On*. My forehead began to burn as my eyes clocked an advert for an event at a place called Ness Botanic Gardens on the Wirral Peninsular, which I'd never even heard of before.

The following Sunday we were about to go for a family walk, when Ness Gardens flashed through my mind again. Luckily, I have a hubby who accepts my spontaneous Sagittarian ways and before long we were all bundled in the car, making the 40-minute drive to our destination.

It was a typical place to walk, with beautiful gardens, a waterfall and a café. And you guessed it – right in the middle of this stunning scenery is a workshop room for hire. It's light and bright, with windows all the way around and doors that open up right into the gardens. Perfect!

I certainly thanked my lucky stars for that one.

3. Project Your Thoughts to Get Noticed

You can also use your star to help you to stand out and be noticed. If you want to be picked for something or want to be remembered, then your star is the perfect tool. Let's say you're going for a job interview and you want to make a really good impression, where you want the board to remember you!

- Focus on your star.

- Visualize it shining brightly in your aura.

- Now, tap in to happy or excited feelings that you'll experience once your desired outcome is a reality.

- Visualize or hear the intended result – such as being congratulated.

- Tune in to the happy emotions of how this manifestation makes you feel.

- Next, transfer this image – or the intention of it – into your star.

- Picture the star exploding in tiny sparks of light, just like a sparkler, sending the energy into your aura as well as the cosmos.

People will be attracted to you, without knowing why. This is because they'll feel the authenticity of a person who follows their soul, for there's nothing more attractive than that.

After you've finished showcasing yourself, just imagine the star dimming down, similar to the previous exercise where we closed down the petals of your chakras.

Congratulations! You've just become acquainted with another beautiful Archeiai. Lady Mary warms my heart every time I think of her. She's so sweet. Please continue to discover her teachings and her wisdom by repeating the practices and then making up your own! There's still so much knowledge within her that she wishes to share with you.

CHAPTER 10

Lady Shekinah
Glory of the Goddess

Lady Shekinah is a fresh-faced Archangel who's recently begun to reveal more of herself to all of us here on Earth. Formally a universal angel – one who governed larger projects within the multiverse – she's currently focusing her energy on Project Earth. Alongside the growing number of Archeiai, she's here to assist with the great rebalance of Earth, in addition to midwifing Gaia through her rebirth.

Her name translates to 'Glory', which is how the whole universe will feel once we've accomplished the mammoth task of stepping into our new golden age. On an individual level, she'll help you to achieve your personal victories. Once accomplished, your only remaining desire will be to serve others, which is the highest attainable glory.

Lady Shekinah is a primal aspect of the Divine feminine, meaning she's one of the oldest emanations of the Goddess in the universe. In our past, highly evolved human beings knew of her angelic existence, but as intended she was erased from our history. Yet, her name wasn't entirely forgotten and appears in various religious and spiritual teachings. She's been known as the 'Glory of God', the 'Dwelling

Place of God', the 'Holy Spirit' and even the 'Female Counterpart of God'. These interpretations are neither right nor wrong. They're merely versions of her multitude of aspects, perceived from the angle at which the observer was standing.

She's here to remind you that the universe or Creator is more than a singular entity. There's no single man or woman sat in the clouds but rather a collective omnipresent energy inherent in everyone and everything. Nor is our Source exclusively male or female. Lady Shekinah helps us to break free from the duality concept, so that we become more deeply accepting of this fundamental truth: the masculine aspect of God is incomplete without its feminine counterpart.

Lady Shekinah can help you to align your personal energy centres with the sacred wisdom held inherent within the land. By planting you firmly in the present, she helps you to lap up each moment, causing you to experience more bliss and ease. She helps you to bridge heaven on Earth.

Lady Shekinah is truly a special angel who'll really bring out the angel in you! She has very selflessly volunteered to serve humanity in several ways. Her key roles covered in this book are:

- the governing and awakening of your Earth Star chakra

- assisting you to remain grounded

- channelling healing energies and ancient wisdom from other planets and dimensions

Lady Shekinah's Appearance

Lady Shekinah reminds me of a galactic priestess. I find her to be very tall and slender. Her huge aura is silver in colour, as is everything else that she 'wears'. Her hair, robes and wings – absolutely everything – is made up of silver metallic light.

Lady Shekinah's Energy

Lady Shekinah's energy is wonderful. If you're blessed to be in her presence, she'll elevate your spirit and open your mind to realization consciousness. From this level of reality, you connect to Source, mind to mind. Source being the container of all wisdom, records and information, with you acting as the antenna, the receiver of Divine revelation.

This intelligence frees up any doubts that you're not worthy or you're a bad person, for when the Lady Shekinah within you awakens, you recognize and reclaim your own divinity. She lifts the veil of separation from 'knowing' that you're Divine to actually feeling it very deeply in your core. You'll literally feel the presence of God/dess, or the Holy Spirit, in every atom of your being and it's a truly beautiful sensation. She'll give you a taster of enlightenment.

Archeia Shekinah is the archetypal Holy Spirit, the breath of Source, the light who resides within every living thing. Her essence threads us together, connecting the dots so that we can experience our individuality while simultaneously being aware of our interwoven realities.

She can help you with:

- activating your Earth Star chakra and teaching you how to use it

- experiencing heaven on Earth

- tapping in to unity consciousness

- balancing your feminine and masculine perceptions and tendencies

- dissolving the illusion of separation

- accepting your divinity

- allowing others to find their own truth

- accepting the Divine plan

- grounding your energy

- feeling Divine

- healing the Earth

- channelling energy from the stars

- accessing wisdom from energy grids

Lady Shekinah's Calling Cards

The following list includes some signs to look out for when you're working with Archeia Shekinah. These calling cards can help you to recognize her whisperings to you. They serve as confirmation that she's by your side:

- Her number vibration is 2112 – the number sequence of the cosmic moment. This number reminds you of your impending golden destiny – the reclaiming of your divinity.

- Lady Shekinah has several power animal totems: the dove – traditionally symbolizing the Holy Spirit; toads – living on both land and water, and representing heaven and Earth; and peacocks – contrary to how we're taught, the white female peacock represents the masculine seed (semen) and the lovely golden 'eye' on the male peacock's feathers represents the female egg (ovum). This role reversal is an analogy. It reminds us that there's masculine in every female and feminine in every male. It also shows that neither sex reigns superior. Without each other, human life ceases to exist. Peacock medicine takes us beyond polarity, even above sexuality.

- Working with Lady Shekinah leaves you with a very contented feeling. Faith is restored as she opens your eyes to the glory and perfection present in all of creation.

- You'll probably feel much more grounded when she's around you. Despite her being a galactic angel, she'll root you firmly into the here and now.

- Her flowers are 'Star Gazer' lilies and caladiums. The Star Gazers represent the Earth Star chakra. Caladiums are nicknamed both 'angel wings' and 'heart of Jesus'. I think that the names of this plant sum up our ascension perfectly: we're here to awaken our Christed heart and gain our angel wings!

- She's also the guardian angel of El Bufo, a potent medicine of the Sonoran Desert toad. Its active ingredient is called the God Molecule or Spirit Molecule. Used only in a very sacred ceremony, a highly initiated shaman will offer you the medicine, allowing you to experience a profound oneness with Source.

Angel of the Earth Star Chakra

Lady Shekinah governs our Earth Star chakra. This is the first chakra in the 12-chakra system. She jokes, 'Before you can gain your wings, you must first gain your Earth Star!' We each have the blueprint of our Earth Star centre within our aura – all we have to do is initiate it. Lady Shekinah can help you to activate this energy centre if you've never worked with it before. If you're already familiar with it, she can certainly increase its light quotient, fine-tuning its capacity to hold more light.

The Earth Star chakra is located about 20–25 centimetres (8–10 inches) below your feet. It can be used as an anchor, grounding your energies to the here and now. Lady Shekinah reminds us of the importance of presence, and how easily you can lose touch with reality when you're working on your spiritual development. Being in the here and now is the key to experiencing heaven on Earth.

Lady Shekinah is very passionate about helping people to feel at home on Planet Earth. Most psychics, indigos and lightworkers have felt like they don't fit into society at some point in their lives. It can be a very lonely place to feel as though you're an outcast or even worse, as if you're the black sheep of the family (like me).

Lady Shekinah can help you to heal these perceptions by realizing the glory in your uniqueness. She'll help you to accept your differences by plugging you into your Earth Star chakra. She adds, 'The number one reason that you don't feel connected or at home on this planet isn't because of your differences but because you are out of touch with nature's rhythms.'

Allowing Lady Shekinah to embed your Earth Star chakra into Mother Earth will establish a deep sense of belonging. Feeling included and part of something creates the basis of a secure psychological foundation. Knowing your true place also adds to the collective healing of the feminine. For far too long we've been put in our place, unable to discover who we really are.

Some men and women are still in resistance, subconsciously not registering that we now have the freedom to be ourselves, and thus failing to express it. Lady Shekinah will teach you to feel comfortable with whoever you are, wherever you are and at whatever stage you're at. She explains that you're in the perfect place for your soul's growth and when your soul feels at home, you'll truly flourish and blossom.

You can also use your Earth Star chakra as an umbilical cord. When connected to Mother Earth, your energy is consistently nourished and replenished. If you can't get your bare feet out in nature every day, this is a perfect alternative to access those negative ions that keep your systems healthy. Quantum physics provides evidence of the phenomenon of the atom being in two places at the same time. Because of your attention (atoms gather in the direction in which you're focusing), atoms out in the soil can create a wormhole – a structure linking disparate points in spacetime – allowing them to dwell in your presence simultaneously.

Angel Encounter

During the 15 years that I was practising as an energy healer, I came to know the angels very well. I was always accompanied by several of them, ranging from spirit guides and loved ones to guardian angels, various Archangels and sometimes Ascended Masters, all dependent upon the healing requirements of the individual. Sometimes my therapy room would be jam-packed, absolutely teaming with light beings all working together.

As time passed and more and more people began to awaken spiritually, my healing sessions evolved. Under the tuition of Archangel Metatron, I began to learn how to tweak my clients' energy bodies, unlock their spiritual gifts and even activate dormant energy centres. When the time came for the higher-dimensional chakras to be reinstated, Lady Shekinah appeared to me with Archangel Metatron.

I was hosting my annual winter retreat in Glastonbury and had just held a water rebirth ceremony at the White Spring – a very holy spring under the Tor. Being submerged into freezing cold water on a November evening is truly magical and exhilarating, but as you can imagine, my guests don't hang about for long afterwards. They always make a dash back to our cosy accommodation to get warm and dry off in preparation for our subsequent celebratory feast. This particular evening was no different. We'd performed a really beautiful ritual and one by one, after dunking the girls, they giddily ran the stone's throw distance back to the house, leaving me to lock the gates.

Alone in the candlelit cave, I paused for a moment to breathe in the magic. The smell of the incense and the sound of water crashing around me made me smile inside. To me, this was paradise. Feeling grateful, I whispered 'Thank you,' to the universe and it seemed that the universe whispered something back, for a silver dazzling light appeared in the centre of the pool. I felt Archangel Metatron appear beside me, but my gaze was transfixed upon this magnificent silver light that had now emerged from the water and was rising right up to the ceiling, eventually forming a female angel.

As soon as I wondered who this was, the answer immediately entered my mind. It was Archangel Shekinah. She beckoned me to come over and stand where she was, in the centre of the freezing pool of water. Without hesitation, I was knee-deep in seconds. I actually stood inside her. Waves of energy rippled through me from head to toe. The current was so strong that I was moving involuntarily. It was like standing in a wind tunnel. Drawn to the power of this loving magnetic force, I surrendered.

Archangel Metatron placed a tiny six-pointed star over my head. Placing his finger at the highest tip of the point, he projected his light, somehow making the star grow larger until it totally encapsulated my entire body. By now, Lady Shekinah was holding the base point of the star, which was located deeply beneath my feet. I became aware of a grey energy centre in this area. I 'understood' it was my Earth Star chakra.

Instinctively, I began to breathe very slowly and intentionally. I somehow knew that I had to 'accept' this activation by breathing it to life. As I did, the grey vortex began to light up, a platinum light radiating outwards, signifying that the activation was now complete. The next step was to anchor it into the Earth, but the angels told me that I needed time to integrate it fully into my energy body for the next three days first. Just when I'd felt that I was so entirely blessed in my life, this amazing experience had occurred. I was high as a kite, brimming with joy.

I don't remember locking up or walking back to the house. I sat at the dining table alone in a daze – the girls had saved me a plate of food. I'd been gone over an hour! I wasn't hungry in the slightest, but Lady Shekinah said, 'Eat.'

My studies with Lady Shekinah and Archangel Metatron began three days later. After about one year, I began offering this activation to some of my clients. If you like, you can also try this exercise later on in the chapter.

Angel of Grounding

Lady Shekinah is the best angel to call in when you're struggling to ground your energy. Basically, you need to be present in the moment to be grounded. She can help you to feel in the here and now, and improve your clarity and your ability to focus, all by simply linking your energy snuggly into the Earth plane.

Because we're enduring a huge evolutionary leap, it's really important to have something for our energy to grasp onto so that we can endure the process without too many complications. Lady Shekinah says that many of you have been experiencing 'ascension symptoms'. These symptoms commonly include: insomnia, headaches, brain fog, vertigo, ringing in the ears, exhaustion, autoimmune disorders, depression and uncontrollable empathy. She says that *all* of these symptoms are made manifest by working within the higher-dimensional planes without grounding your energy efficiently. In effect, you're becoming a new species, a superhuman.

These symptoms can be avoided entirely. I for one haven't experienced any ascension symptoms since I began to follow Lady Shekinah's advice. She taught me how to really ground myself after any psychic and spiritual work. This also included releasing excess energy by sending it out through the soles of my feet. As I mentioned before, excess energy becomes stagnant, thus manifesting in dis-ease.

To reap the benefits of working with Lady Shekinah, try the Earthing techniques that follow later in this chapter.

Angel of Energy Grids

Lady Shekinah pumps high-vibrational light into the dragon lines in the ground. These ancient pathways are the meridians of Mother Earth. Just as our energy pathways become blocked with injury and trauma, so do hers through our drilling and polluting. Mother Earth, Gaia, can clear out her energetic system all by herself. A volcano eruption, earthquake or flood will easily dissipate heavy energy that needs clearing.

However, these destructive forces are disastrous to us and all of the other creatures who are touched by it. Lady Shekinah says that with our prayers, and by raising our vibrational frequency and drawing down light, we can help to prevent further natural disasters from occurring by clearing up the land. We're the endangered species, not the Earth, so it's up to us to restore balance to her ecosystems if we want to keep this place our home.

If you're concerned about global warming, call upon Lady Shekinah and Archangel Sandalphon to assign helper angels to protect specific vulnerable areas such as melting ice caps. Similarly, if there's a flood or a storm, Lady Shekinah can carry your prayers to these angels to see if they can negotiate with Gaia for another way to purge the land.

Lady Shekinah says that many areas of our planet need clearing. Just think of all the wars, suffering and death – our stories are written in the land. On a more positive note, the wisdom of our ancestors is also buried within the ground, hidden in mountains and energy lines (ley lines) below. Once we've cleared the layers of debris, all of the wisdom is ours to be reclaimed.

Lightworkers have already started with the big clean-up. Our hidden gems are seeping into the surface of the land and out into our oceans, bringing blessings of wisdom to all. If you're interested in helping to clear the energy grids on Earth, Lady Shekinah will lead you. She says that life on Earth is give and take. It's good to give something back and you also store up a few brownie points in the karmic bank.

It's a very simple process. First, think of the qualities you'd like to impart upon our planet. Then choose a planet that could gift that quality to Earth.

You could choose:

- Venus for love

- Mercury for clearer communication

- Sun for joy

- Moon for illuminating the negative shadow influences, such as revealing corruption within governments and unethical companies

- Chiron for releasing the old paradigm

- Jupiter for truth and education

- Sirius for ascension energies

Meditate on it or conduct some research online. Once you have a gift in mind for the planet, send your chakra column up towards your chosen planet. Respectfully ask permission to take energy while thinking of the quality or virtue that you're blessing the Earth with. For example, if you've plugged into Venus, you may think of the word love. Finally, release the gift of energy into Earth via your Earth Star chakra, always giving thanks before disconnecting.

You can tailor this process to whatever you see fit, as long as it's for a good cause. You could send wisdom into Parliament, or love to a cause or country. Lady Shekinah says that you can also call upon the planetary influences to rebalance your home or work. What amazing things we're accomplishing together with our angel family guiding us!

The Earth Stars Duo

Lady Shekinah's twin flame is Archangel Sandalphon. But as Archangel Sandalphon is a twin angel with Archangel Metatron, the bond between these angels is very closely formed. In fact, Lady Shekinah works with Archangel Metatron just as much, if not more, as she does with Archangel Sandalphon. This is because their energies reflect the primary forces of Yin and Yang.

Lady Shekinah and Archangel Metatron are the marriage of heaven and Earth. Lady Shekinah and Archangel Sandalphon are the masculine and feminine of Earth. Archangels Seraphina and Metatron are the masculine and feminine of heaven.

Together, they're the elements of all creation:

- Metatron being Air

- Seraphina being Fire

- Shekinah being Water

- Sandalphon being Earth

- The fifth element being the spirit of the unified field (God/dess)

Lady Shekinah and Archangel Sandalphon govern the Earth Star chakra and together they ground deeply into the Earth the high energies of heaven from Archangels Metatron and Lady Seraphina. Archangel Sandalphon distributes the ascension energies into the trees, plants and crystals that grow within the Earth, while Lady Shekinah focuses on us and our rivers and oceans. They hold the light frequency of the platinum ray and direct the angels of 'the word' or the 'Divine Word' to anchor angelic blessings from above.

The etheric portal of these archangels is Mount Kailash, Tibet. This sacred mountain is a physical body of wisdom. Mystics and yogis from around the globe make a pilgrimage to get up close to the mountain. It's believed that the secrets of the universe reside within it. It's even said that Lord Krishna disappeared up the mountain; some say he went there to die, while others believe he's still alive up there. This safe haven has been protected from our cosmic knowledge until we become evolved enough to use it with love and wisdom. With the use of your Earth Star chakra, you can travel to sacred locations as such, where the Masters will impart their Earth wisdom upon you.

Archangel Sandalphon

Archangel Sandalphon is a lovely, gentle angel. His presence is very calming and relaxing. He's a great angel to help you to be in the here and now. Being the angel of music, he reminds you of all of the ways in which music can lighten up your day. He's the angel who'll prompt your favourite song to play on the radio when you're feeling down and he's also the guardian of the sacred shamanic songs called icaros, which are thought of as living prayers. If you're learning to play an instrument, ask Archangel Sandalphon to guide you to play from the heart. If you hold drum ceremonies or chant, call him in. The angels of the Divine Word will come and join you, spreading your light into the world.

If you're an empath, or sensitive and loud sounds are very uncomfortable and harsh on your spirit, you can ask Archangel Sandalphon to filter out the vibrations. Simply imagine sending irritable feelings out though the soles of your feet and he'll safely dispose of them for you.

Working with Lady Shekinah

When I'm working with Lady Shekinah I like to wear silver or white clothes and If I'm creating an altar, I'll chose those same colours for my candles. The perfect energetically aligned essential oils are angelica and sandalwood. I've also taken drops of the Star of Bethlehem Bach remedy to heighten my awareness from time to time. Please check with your GP or pharmacist if you're on any medication.

Lady Shekinah's Gemstones

The following crystals have the healing vibrations that resonate with the work of Lady Shekinah:

- desert rose

- selenite

- a star-shaped clear quartz

- labradorite

- lithium quartz

- smoky quartz

These gemstones are high vibrational. They'll raise your consciousness to the stars, quite literally. They already contain secrets of the universe within them, but Lady Shekinah will help you to decipher their wisdom. Simply wear or hold the gemstones during your meditations. When you feel ready, try the following invocation to experience Lady Shekinah's energy:

 ## INVOCATION: CALLING IN LADY SHEKINAH

Once your altar is all set (optional), you're ready to invoke the beautiful Lady Shekinah:

You will need:

~ a pen and a piece of paper

~ a white candle

~ incense or essential oils to keep the energy in the room clear

Start by dedicating your candle:

~ Say, 'Lady Shekinah, Lady Shekinah, Lady Shekinah.'

~ Light your candle.

~ State her invocation below three times.

~ With your hands in the prayer position, say, 'Holy Spirit, flow through my veins. Lady Shekinah your sacred name, bless me this day, bless me this night. May I rise into glory by following your light.'

~ Gently lower your eyes and take slow, deliberate breaths.

~ Allow yourself to experience Lady Shekinah's energy.

~ Without analysing, be aware of any physical sensations, messages or visions.

~ Write down your experience.

~ Before you blow out your candle, ask Lady Shekinah to give you a clear confirmation sign in the physical world over the next few days.

~ Give thanks to Lady Shekinah.

Lady Shekinah will help you to feel the Holy Spirit – the Divine breath of Source that's inherent in all things including yourself. By silencing your mind when working with her, you become more open to receiving. She's more likely to offer you her teachings through feelings rather than a visual message, so trust what emotions arise when you call her into your space.

Whether you feel spiritually advanced or not, it's worth integrating the Earth Star chakra. You may be inclined to leave the Soul Star, Causal and Stellar gateway chakras for now while you work on solidifying the lower chakras, which is essential. However, the Earth Star chakra will really help you to get to grips with mastering all of your earthly challenges, such as work, family, romance, finances and so forth. That's why I've included this next exercise in this book, as it'll help everyone:

ACTIVATING YOUR EARTH STAR CHAKRA

There are optimal timeframes for practising this exercise. If you're reading this anywhere near the times of solstice or the eclipse, save it for then! If not and you're raring to get going, I'd do this on the next full moon. I'd definitely set up an altar or make an offering for the angels for this exercise, as this one's a biggie.

Make sure you're familiar with the location of this chakra before you start. The Earth Star chakra lies about 20–25 centimetres (8–10 inches) below your feet. It's in direct alignment with your chakra column, so if you drew a straight line through the middle of your body, all of the seven chakras are positioned on this line.

~ Preferably standing (or sitting upright), expand your fingers and toes then loosely begin to shake them.

~ Start to shake your entire body for a good few minutes to get your energy flowing.

~ Loudly chant in Lady Shekinah by saying, 'Shh-ay-keeey-naaah' seven times.

~ Now, you've generated a lot of energy.

~ You feel the Divine power of the Holy Spirit vibrating throughout you.

~ A pillar of silver light rises through the centre of the Earth.

~ It's directed towards you from Lady Shekinah herself.

~ Her silver angels flutter around the pillar of light.

~ Imagine the pillar now hitting your Earth Star chakra, sending a powerful vibration all the way up your body.

~ As it does so, take a quick, deep breath in through the nose and a slow breath out through the mouth.

~ Visualize your grey Earth Star chakra lighting up with the jolt of light.

~ It now begins to glow silver.

~ Mentally ask Archangel Shekinah to hold this light for you for the coming days or weeks while you adjust to it.

~ Once it's fully integrated, you can use it as you do other chakra centres.

~ Disconnect your energy from the pillar.

~ Imagine the light of your newly activated chakra dimming down until you're ready to work with it again.

~ Give thanks to your angel helpers.

You may experience very little or a lot during this process. Remember, you're at the perfect stage of your spiritual growth, so don't be disheartened if you don't see, hear or feel all that much at first. The more time you spend developing your inner awareness, the sharper it'll become. Congratulate yourself for having a go regardless of depth or enlightening moments. Trust your process. The universe gives you what's perfect for your needs, not what you 'want'.

As I mentioned earlier, Lady Shekinah can really help you to get grounded and focused by centring your Earth Star chakra into the Earth. As this energy centre is transpersonal (outside the body), it's naturally in contact with the ground without even trying. However, you must exercise the chakra, otherwise it'll literally just be collecting dust.

GROUNDING YOUR ENERGY WITH THE EARTH STAR CHAKRA

Here are a few tips to help you to get started with the Earth Star chakra:

Each morning, activate your Earth Star chakra as follows:

~ Start with your spine straight and palms open by your sides.

~ Focus your awareness on the Earth Star chakra and visualize it lighting up like a beautiful silver disc.

~ Imagine anchoring it in place central to your chakra column.

~ Think of your goals for the day ahead.

~ Your thought activates a network of silver electrical pulses that travel from your brain all the way down to your Earth Star chakra.

~ The pulses (network of messages) infuse your visualization into the Earth Star chakra – which will help you to stay on course to achieving your goal.

Rather than sending grounding roots into the Earth via the Root chakra, try sending them out through the Earth Star chakra. It makes sense that now we're granted access to higher-dimensional energies, we need higher-dimensional chakras to carry this volume of light. Think of the Earth Star chakra as having the same grounding functions as the Root, only the Root is like your five-year-old laptop and the Earth Star is like a brand-new, top-of-the-range piece of technology – it's much more efficient.

Additionally, the Root chakra is no longer as effective for grounding, as it contains all of our personal fears and ancestral karma. Use the Root chakra for this reason: to heal your fears and release your ancestral karma. Leave the Earth Star chakra to deal with grounding cosmic energies and to trailblaze your wishes into reality.

Keeping it clean

It's well known that low-vibrational energy is denser (heavier) than light, bright energy. For this reason, negative energy tends to accumulate lower down, close to the ground. With this in mind, it's a sensible idea to flush your Earth Star chakra regularly, as it's the most likely to encounter negativity energy. Embrace rather than fear this in any way. Just think of it as similar to how you wipe your feet when you've been outside.

When you feel as though you could benefit from releasing some tense and nervous energy, try the following exercise:

- ~ If possible, stand outside barefoot.

- ~ Imagine your silver disc lighting up and spinning anticlockwise, sending energy outwards.

- ~ Now, imagine black energy beginning to pour out of it like a watering can.

- ~ Keep going until it eventually runs clear.

- ~ Clear the energy from the ground afterwards by invoking the Violet Flame (for a recap, see Chapter 2 – Holy Amethyst).

- ~ You can refill the energies of the Earth Star chakra by linking it into power points on Earth (see the exercise that follows).

This energy-flushing exercise given to me by Lady Shekinah is both short and sweet. It's a perfect little technique when you're on the go and encounter a feeling of becoming spiritually 'dirty'. I felt like that after receiving a massage from a woman who'd offloaded her problems onto me during the treatment. Her toxic energy had been kneaded into my body and her aura was of course in very close contact with mine as she was physically touching me. Being an empath, I knew I'd feel dreadful if I failed to shift the energy immediately. I simply sat in my car and flushed my Earth Star chakra. The energy cleared as simply as that.

You can also use your Earth Star chakra to tap in to secret knowledge that's stored within the land anywhere in the world without leaving your home. This is because when you're working on spirituality, you're working within the inner dimensions, so the external senses such as ears and eyes are irrelevant. In fact, they can be a hindrance to your development most of the time, in that your physical eyes expect and judge.

COLLECTING ANCIENT WISDOM WITH YOUR EARTH STAR CHAKRA

Ancient wisdom is buried within power points (energy vortices) in the land. When your Earth Star chakra is active you can tap in to the high-vibrational frequencies of these lands without actually visiting them. If you feel drawn to a particular civilization, ask Lady Shekinah to take you there with this exercise. The Earth Star chakra can transcend time and space, so you're free to explore any period since the beginning of time. If you've always felt drawn to ancient Egypt or the temples at Angkor Wat, Cambodia, here's your chance!

You will need:

~   a pen and a piece of paper

~   a white candle

~   a bundle of earthy dried herbs such as mugwort

First, pass the smoke of the herbs through your aura to clear your space before you begin:

~   Light the candle.

~   Invoke Lady Shekinah by placing your hands into the prayer posture.

~   Call her name three times.

~   Say, 'Lady Shekinah, Lady Shekinah, Lady Shekinah.'

~   Ask her to wrap your Earth Star chakra in the light of her platinum ray.

~   Imagine this area igniting by lighting up.

~   Say the name of your destination three times.

~   Be specific, such as the Great Sphinx of Giza in Egypt.

~   Chant 'Om' very slowly seven times while keeping your focus on the Earth Star chakra.

~ Send your consciousness through the Earth Star chakra and Lady Shekinah will travel with you.

~ You come to a platinum door.

~ You're greeted by the wisdom guardians of this land.

~ Allow yourself the freedom to explore this sacred place, taking note of all that you sense, smell, see, taste or hear.

~ When you're ready, bring your Earth Star chakra back into the room by focusing on your surroundings.

~ Wiggle your fingers and toes and open your eyes.

~ Ensure you write down all you discovered.

~ Thank Lady Shekinah and the guardians of the lands to which you travelled.

It's fine if it doesn't make sense to you now. Like receiving pieces of a jigsaw puzzle, it will do at some point in the future. That's why it's a great idea to take notes to reflect upon your visions in the future.

You can travel the inner planes of the Earth to your heart's content. Your spirit is beyond space and time. Just imagine all of the exciting places that you can travel to and receive the wisdom of their cultures. You could ask to visit the Aboriginal lands, the Amazon rainforest, the Tibetan mountains, the Archangels' physical retreats – the world is your oyster.

Lady Shekinah can help you to integrate upgraded ascension tools, such as the Earth Star chakra, into your daily life while simultaneously ensuring that you remain grounded. You're free to explore way beyond Earth. With her protection you can visit all dimensions and universes. What an incredible age to be experiencing a human incarnation! Enjoy your travels with Lady Shekinah…

CHAPTER 11

Lady Seraphina
Fire of the Goddess

Lady Seraphina is currently the highest ranking of all of the female angels who work with us here on Earth. She's not technically an Archangel; she actually belongs to an order of very high-dimensional angels known as the seraphim.

Lady Seraphina's name means 'Feminine Essence of the Seraphim'. She's the female 'Fire Serpent of the Goddess'.

The seraphim withdraw from Earth for long periods of time to let us go about living our lives while they work on more universal matters. However, they always return when we're approaching a new golden age. At the time of writing this book, that time is now, and for at least the next 25 years, Lady Seraphina is waiting to assist. She can help you to:

- heal your energy pathways

- clear the patterns of patriarchy

- become the Divine Word

Lady Seraphina's Appearance

Lady Seraphina is pure energy and like all of the angels, she makes herself 'look' humanistic for our comfort and ability to understand. In the main, we try to perceive the angels through our five senses, yet this isn't how to truly see an angel. An angel is perceived in its truest form through our heart, but as we're still apprentices in terms of working on this level, they continue to give us visual experiences to remember!

In the Bible, the seraphim are described as having six wings, but I perceive them in a different way. I recognize Lady Seraphina as an outline of an angel with a large red-and-gold flame extending throughout her centre. Surrounding the flame, her energy body looks like moving crystal-clear water. The best way to describe the appearance of her energy body is like water or a mirage surrounding her. Sometimes she extends her flame to create a circle of fire around herself or others.

Lady Seraphina's Energy

Lady Seraphina's energy will simply blow you away. The first time you encounter her is a big 'wow' moment – well it was for me, anyway.

Her presence is all-encompassing. She expands not just though the external world but within every atom of your existence, from the beginning to the end of time, including everything that lies between. You really get to experience the timeless essence of your soul during precious moments shared with Lady Seraphina.

Lady Seraphina is beyond archetype. She's the mother of all feminine archetypes. All goddesses, angels, beings, qualities and aspects of the Divine feminine emanate from her. They're like the stream and rivers while Lady Seraphina is the ocean.

She can help you with:

- healing your energy with words and sound

- developing your light body

- igniting the Divine feminine flame

- reclaiming your feminine energy aspects

- cleansing the past of patriarchy

- ascending and descending the DNA ladder

- experiencing your timeless essence

- reclaiming the power of the Divine Word

- rekindling your Divine spark

- shedding your skin of your false self

- identifying your original woundings

Lady Seraphina's Calling Cards

Lady Seraphina has her own set of unique calling cards. Seeing these validates her presence and captures your attention towards her when she has a message to share with you:

- You may notice her energetic number sequence, which is any formation of 144, the number 144,000 being sacred. Revelations speak about the vast army of 144,000 to have 'received the seal of the Father on their forehead'. It states that the 114,000 are 12,000 people from each of the 12 tribes of Israel that 'have a special relationship with the lamb' – Jesus.

- In yogi traditions, there are 72,000 nadis on each side of the body, half female and half male. If united, these numbers total

144,000. Similarly, the five lower chakras (Root to Throat) have a combined 48 petals. Adding the 96 petals of the Third Eye chakra totals 144 petals. To then add on the 1,000-petal lotus of the Crown chakra totals 144,000. I believe that this number contains the secret to the Divine marriage of male and female, of mind, body and spirit. Lady Seraphina can help you to achieve this number coding, and to clear and activate every energy centre in the body, completing your soul in every way.

- Her animals are snakes and of course dragons, which are seen in mythology as 'giant serpents'.

- You're likely to recognize your divinity on many levels like never before when you're in her holy presence. You'll be left savouring the boundless space of infinite love.

- Your heart will overflow with love and gratitude as you transcend the realms of the mind. Small stresses become a thing of the past once you've had a taste of a much grander picture.

- Her flowers are Parrot's Beak lotus – resembling the Divine flame and the Divine Word. Although these flowers are native to the Canary Islands, they will still cross your path in some way. The rarity of her flower makes this calling card all the more undeniable of her presence.

WHO ARE THE SERAPHIM?

The seraphim translates in Hebrew as 'The Fiery Ones'. It's said that this name derives from their fiery passion for doing God's work. Yet, I suspect that like most things, there's a much deeper meaning to the name of these celestial beings. The word 'seraph' is a singular term and seraphim is the plural. Interestingly, seraph is used interchangeably throughout the Bible, also being the same word for serpent. The seraph is the ancient symbol of the Divine feminine and the energetic alchemy of a kundalini rising.

In the Bible, seraphim are described as having six wings, two to cover their feet, two to cover their face and two with which to fly. In Isaiah 6:1-8, the seraphim sing 'Holy Holy Holy' beneath the ark or throne of God. With a piece of hot coal from the altar of the Lord, they anoint the lips of the prophet Isaiah (a self-confessed man of unclean lips, verse 5). Without burning him, he's cleansed from his perceived sin and made whole (holy) once again. I can only speculate that Isaiah is being anointed with the Word.

The seraphim are the most highly ascended order of angels. We're very lucky to be able to communicate with them as it's quite rare. They're helping us to usher in the new age, by igniting the flame of Source within.

The seraphim are also helping us to purify old patterns embedded deep within the planet. They have dragonlike qualities that can purify deeply into dense areas. They've even been known to save souls from hell (Naraka, purgatory or dimensions of lost or fragmented souls), restoring beings to a state of glory. On a humanistic level, they can teach us to become like a snake. Rather than continuously peeling the layers of the onion, she teaches us to shed our skin all at once, allowing us that rare opportunity to advance.

Angel of 144,000

Lady Seraphina can help you on your journey back to wholeness, to clear and fire up your 144,000 energy pathways that activate your sacred seal, granting you access to heaven or wholeness.

The Dalai Lama said, 'If you think you're too small to make a difference, try sleeping with a mosquito in the room.' We all know how this tiny insect can have a massive effect on us if we get that teeny bite. The itching is relentless. Similarly, if one of your tiny little nadis become obstructed, your ego mind will itch away at you until you come to realize what wants clearing and why.

It's so easy to discover your blockages. Simply follow the trail of negative thoughts and physical symptoms. During a meditative state, ask yourself what your body is trying to reveal to you – the answer will always come! Ask Lady Seraphina to help you to reclaim the vibrancy of all of your energy pathways. Not only is this essential to having good health, but it's also key in unifying your soul with the Creator. Remember, half of your energy centres are masculine and the other half feminine. With most of us more dominantly working from one side, it takes time to integrate your other half.

When your mind, body and spirit is in unison, you literally become lighter. Your carbon body starts to become crystalline. The number of the beast, '666', can be interpreted as our carbon-body illusion, keeping us in our own hell. Carbon-12, one of five elements in the human DNA, is composed of six protons, six electrons and six neutrons. When we're free from our 144,000 (potential) restraints, we're free from suffering. Relax, this is very deep content and the angels don't expect you to learn or understand it all. They'll always ensure that you're provided with the life lessons that you need in order to maintain your 144,000 pathways – which open the gateway to God/dess.

Angel of Core Wounding

We all have a core wounding – that's what enables us to experiment within our individual reality. This wound drives us to seek wholeness by reuniting with God, or even by seeking union in a romantic partner.

Lady Seraphina knows how we feel because she's experienced this, too. In fact, all beings who have an identity have gone through this process. When we first originate as a being separate from our

Creator, it's inevitable that we feel a sense of disengagement on some level.

When I was regressed to remember my first past-life incarnation, to the bemusement of my hypnotherapist I described myself as a 'Divine spark'. However, as much as I felt my divinity, I still craved to be reunited with Source and went into great detail about 'the split' being my first ever broken heart.

This is our original 'origin' wound, when we became a branch from the tree of life. We left our Eden with Source and then branched out from our 'other half' to experience our creativity in the world.

Lady Seraphina can help you to accept your original wounds. She reminds you that in your carbon body, you're limited. But this is exactly what the proverbial doctor ordered. This is your perfect opportunity to embrace a unique expression of Source. Creator witnesses itself through your eyes! That's how important you are.

Angel of Numbers

Call upon Lady Seraphina to help you to realize your own higher aspect and to nurture your own original wound. She empathizes with us. Some sensitive souls suffer so much that they literally feel homesick, but in truth there's nowhere to 'go' – it's a matter of reclaiming and awakening.

Being so close to the Creator, Lady Seraphina has a unique gift: she's both an individual seraph and the collective Divine feminine seraphim at the same time. Think of your physical body – scientists estimate that only 10 per cent of you is actually you and the other 90 per cent is made up of cells that collaborate on behalf of you.

Similarly, Lady Seraphina merges with a whole host of seraphim who function independently of her, but all with the same goal. All of the feminine seraphim emanate from her. She urges you to try this gift out for yourselves. She reminds you that compounding your own energy with others' is incredibly powerful, especially when women gather in a circle. This is when miracles occur. Lady Seraphina can help you to join forces with other lightworkers. You'll find that you all bounce off each other, enhancing your magical healing powers and filling in the gap of separation. Separation isn't your original form, unity is.

Angel Encounter

Lady Seraphina is the newest of all of my angel friends. There's so little known about her because she's been working away from Earth since the last Golden Age of Atlantis. Meeting her was one of the most magical experiences of my life and it was only recently.

I was on a retreat in the Lake District, Cumbria, in around 2016. It was close to Easter, but that weekend it snowed heavily. Driving along the narrow country roads back from the monastery, I could hardly see anything for the thick, whirling blizzards that danced all around me, leaving a deep carpet of snow across the land. It truly was a magical scene and it added to the significance of the events that had occurred that weekend.

I'd just received an initiation into the Sisterhood of the Rose and declared myself Priestess of Maria Magdalena (Mary Magdalene). It felt appropriate that as I was being purified internally – my soul kindled by the hearth of Magdalene's flame – the external world was simultaneously being blessed with the pure white snow (as within, so without).

When my visibility became totally obscured by the blizzard, I had no choice but to pull the car over until it was safe to continue. I was in no way afflicted by this situation; I had all the time in the world. Truth be told, I was really enjoying observing the elements in their extreme - it was enlivening. With not a soul or building in sight for miles, I sat in the silence, reflecting upon how very humble and grateful I was to witness such a beautiful moment.

I felt inspired to express my thanks and began to pray. I often meditate directly after prayer and this morning was the same. As I bathed my spirit in the boundless moment, I soon got the urge to write. I recognized it immediately as a sign – someone new wanted to communicate with me. An initial dialogue often came about like this. Rifling through the glove box, I found an envelope to take down the message. I wrote: 'Have you seen her, Seraphina?', the Chi-lites song 'Have You Seen Her' playing in my mind.

I became aware of a presence. I closed my eyes and in my Third Eye chakra, I had a vision of the beloved Mary Magdalene herself. She said nothing, but her gaze spoke a thousand words. I learned of her life, the fall of the feminine and, more importantly, her rising.

Then she spoke:

'Have you seen her?'

I psychically replied, 'Seen who?'

'Seraphina!' she laughed.

'No, I don't think so,' I admitted.

'Would you like to?' Mary Magdalene proceeded to ask.

My reply to which was, 'I'd love to.'

Mary Magdalene kneeled down in the glistening snow, hands in prayer position. A small yellow flower appeared in her hands. She placed it in the snow. The flower began to grow a deep red in colour, so that it now almost resembled a flame. The flame caught the end of Mary Magdalene's dress and began to form a circle of fire all around her, similar to how Lord Shiva is often depicted. Then four golden angels appeared beside her and instantaneously, they all merged together and became one.

This huge angel looked like a fire but moved like water. She spoke:

Your next step is to learn to perceive yourself not as one but as all. Beneath the veil of amnesia, your heart knows this truth. When you fully understand this concept, you will see your reflection in the face of every living thing. Know this and know that this is the task thy set for oneself. A new era approaches. Humanity learn to unite.

I asked the being who she was, as she looked different from all of the other angels I'd seen before. 'I am Seraphina,' she answered. And just like that, Mary Magdalene and Lady Seraphina were both gone.

I got out of the car and looked around, bemused. There was nothing and no one as far as the eye could see. The bitter wind stung my ears. I said aloud, 'Give me a sign that this was real.' The blizzard now calm, it was safe to drive off.

The next day I was chatting on the phone to my dear friend Josie. As usual, we were sharing our adventures of the weekend. She casually mentioned that she'd bought her granddaughter a big white toy cat that walks. 'She called it Seraphina,' she laughed. My heart swelled with thanks.

Angel of Sacred Sound

Lady Seraphina directs the angels of the Divine Word. From her heavenly dimension, these sweet angels carry vibrations of sound through the physical realms, where they can alchemize from spirit to matter. It's well known that most people are underusing one of their most potent superpowers: the sound of their voice.

You're probably well aware of the power in your words. These days, most of us know about the power of affirmations. But Lady Seraphina urges you to remember the immense power in the vibration of the word and how it sounds. How a word physically materializes is dependent upon the energy in which it's spoken to life (how you feel when speaking).

You can experience the potent healing of sound by attending a sound bath or trying kirtan yoga. You can even download healing sound frequencies specifically to resonate with each of the chakras, known as solfeggio. But Lady Seraphina says that it can be more empowering for you to use the power of your voice to make the sounds yourself.

It's said that the entire universe was created by sound. Some yogis believe that 'Om' is that sound. Similarly, in the Bible, the opening chapter to the Gospel of John 1:1 says, 'In the beginning was the Word.' So, what is 'the word' and how is this relevant to you?

The angels of the Divine Word use sound to manifest. These heavenly beings oscillate between the seraphim and Earth, carrying with them the songs of creation. They deliver them directly to Lady Shekinah, who will embed the angelic frequencies into the ley lines on our planet. You've been blessed with the greatest gift of all in terms of creation: your voice. You see, words and sounds contain the very spark of creation within them, too.

Lady Seraphina can help you to choose your words wisely and also help you to pray. She's the Angel of Light Language. Ask her to bless your Throat chakra if you'd like to have a bash at speaking in tongues. Toning is also very effective at healing your body, as it facilitates the release of tension, thus dissipating energy blockages as your energy becomes free moving. If you can't physically speak then try writing down the words or imagine them in your mind.

Our words create magic. When we write words, we learn to spell. Lady Seraphina can help you to realize your manifesting potential through the correct use of words.

The Fiery Duo

Lady Seraphina's twin ray angel is called Archangel Seraphiel. These bright sparks use the flame of Source to purify the darkness and to reawaken the light that's in all beings. Archangel Seraphiel manages the Archangels. Think of him as a commander and Lady Seraphina as the manager of the Archeiai. Usually, the seraphim leave the Archangels to it, so the Archangels can get on with assisting with Earth directly. However, Lady Seraphina volunteers to help out here and there, especially when the Divine feminine now needs an extra boost.

Archangel Seraphiel

Archangel Seraphiel's name translates to 'The Flame of God'. He's also known as the 'Prince of the High Angelic Order'. He has very little direct contact with beings on Earth. Information from Archangel Seraphiel usually comes through Archangel Metatron, who's his second-in-command. They liaise with each other on how the angels can support Earth.

He's one of the main protectors of 'the light'. He directs streams of powerful cleansing Fire energy to maintain the pureness of Source's love. He's more well known in Eastern traditions than in the West. He's known to some as the angel to call upon in case of a fire breaking out. It's said in some texts that Archangel Seraphiel teaches the seraphim the Divine songs. Again, we're brought back to the vibration of sound and words.

You're welcome to pray to Archangel Seraphiel and he'll hear you, but it's unlikely you'll be able to tune in to receive guidance directly. Therefore, it's usually Archangel Metatron or Lady Seraphina who'll be the ones to answer your call.

Working with Lady Seraphina

When I work with this lovely angel, I like to set out my altar just for her. For Lady Seraphina, I'd use a red or gold altar cloth, yellow candles and perhaps a small statue of a snake. I also burn dragon's blood resin; it smells divine and invokes the inner serpent within.

Lady Seraphina's Gemstones

The following crystals have the healing vibrations that resonate with the work of Lady Seraphina:

- seraphinite
- ruby
- septarian
- serpentine
- dragon's blood Jasper

By holding or wearing any of the listed gemstones you can more easily achieve a clearer connection to Lady Seraphina's presence. They're very cleansing stones that can attune you to the element of Fire. They'll awaken qualities such as passion and vigour within you. Now you've learned the basics of this magnificent seraph, you may feel ready to invoke her with the following exercise:

Invocation: Calling in Lady Seraphina

Call upon Lady Seraphina to help you to clear, purify and evolve every microcosm of your soul.

You may like to use the altar items listed earlier in this chapter, as altars help you to create an 'altered' state of awareness. They also show respect and gratitude to all of the elements and the being who supports your growth. Schedule in some quiet time so that you can go deeply within yourself without being distracted.

Lady Seraphina's energy will enter from your Stellar Gateway chakra, your galactic halo that resides about 15–20 centimetres (6–8 inches) above the crown of the head. It's much easier to digest her powerful, pure energy with the vibration of sound. When you chant, try to feel your voice vibrating through you. This will raise your awareness and integrate high energies into your sphere.

You will need:

~ a pen and a piece of paper

~ a white candle

~ one of the previously listed crystals in the section on Lady Seraphina's gemstones

Before you begin, light the white candle then call in Lady Seraphina:

~ Whisper, 'Lady Seraphina, Lady Seraphina, Lady Seraphina.'

~ With your hands in the prayer posture, say, 'Queen of Fire, set my soul alight, cleansing me with your sacred flame upon the chant of thy holy name.'

~ Hold the crystal in cupped hands, gently relaxing them on your lap.

~ With your spine straight, focus your awareness above the crown of your head and slowly chant 'Se-ra-fee-naah' seven times.

~ Feel her energy beginning to blend with yours as she holds your Stellar Gateway chakra between her palms.

~ Her sacred flame begins to burn away limiting beliefs that have been 'placed' over you, both in this lifetime and in past lives.

~ Listen to any guidance that she may have for you.

~ It may come as an idea or a vision, but this is your chance to ask Lady Seraphina any questions that you may have regarding the next steps of your growth.

~ Take time to integrate this high-vibrational energy by daydreaming or relaxing in nature.

~ Ground your energy by digging your heels into the floor.

~ Place your crystal in a safe place and use it again when connecting to Lady Seraphina.

~ Take down notes or messages from your experience.

~ Give thanks to both Lady Seraphina and your guides.

Our Earth's history is embedded in the soil upon which we walk. While many forces of light affix a new blueprint over Earth, one of balance and harmony, human consciousness still continues to reject a higher reality by being trapped in their be-LIE-f patterns. Unconsciously they serve as anchors, digging their heels deep into the old patriarchal paradigms. I make this statement with compassion, not with blame or any sense of superiority; after all, each of us is but a mirror of our own reflection. The issues of Earth belong to us all.

You can help to clear the paradigms of the past of our patriarchs by healing yourself, your land and your ancestral lineage. Try this next exercise to help to contribute to the evolution of human consciousness:

CLEARING INHERITED PATRIARCHAL PARADIGMS

Here's an exercise that you can use to clear embedded patterns that may be lurking in both your subconscious mind and in your ancestral lineage. The first part of this exercise requires some journalling, so grab yourself a pen and notepad, and a hot drink if you wish.

Write these questions at the top of the piece of paper:

1. (In your interpretation), what does your father believe about women?

    Examples:

    Here, I may write things like: My father thought that women are more intelligent than men, yet they belong in the kitchen.

    Or: My father was a womanizer who looked at women as sexual objects. He married several times and believed that all women were just after his money.

    Or: My father adored my mother and he treated her like a queen. He lived for her.

    Write down as many beliefs that you think your father has about women. If your father has been absent from your life, use the closest male family member who's older than you, such as a grandad or uncle.

2. (In your interpretation), what does your mother believe about women?

    Examples:

    Here, I may write things like: My mum said that women are bitchy.

    Or: My mum believes that women find a rich man, get married and make a home.

    Or: My mum believes that all men are b**tards – you should never trust a man!

Again, if your mum hasn't been a part of your life, use this on your closest maternal role model. Extend this list to your grandparents or influential aunts, teachers and so on.

3.   Now, write down the beliefs you have about men and women. I'm sure that your views are very different from theirs, yet subconsciously you'll have inherited some of these beliefs.

4.   When you've written them down, who do you hear talking? Subconsciously, do your answers sound like the be-LIE-fs of your grandparents? Parents? Teachers?

5.   Take all of your negative conditioned beliefs and see if you can trace back to where they originated. Remember, we're looking at your beliefs about men and women, but you can tailor the exercise to clear up any beliefs in the next exercise.

When you have all of your findings written down, it's time to process, transform and then heal these unhelpful paradigms. This next phase of the exercise can be a bit of a lengthy process, especially if you have a big family, so ensure you set aside plenty of time.

THE BIG CLEAN-UP

Clearing up inherited be-LIE-fs is a wonderful practice. This exercise can empower you to summon the courage to stand in your power and live the life that you desire, free from the fear of what others may believe or think. Setting yourself free can also be seen as an offering of healing to the world, as well as a gift to yourself. Your personal empowerment is needed – be a living example of a woman in her power.

You will need:

~ a pen and a piece of paper

~ incense or resin, such as frankincense, to burn

~ a white candle

~ matches

~ a small gift (such as a favourite item) for the person whose beliefs you're clearing; for example, my father loved whisky, so perhaps a small shot of whisky, or a few of my mother's favourite daffodils, my grandad's beloved caramel toffees and so on.

Take a ritual bath. Clear your space by burning your incense and then create an angel altar or whatever you feel best marks the importance of this work so that you can honour those who assist.

~ Light your candle.

~ Call in Lady Seraphina.

~ Say, 'Lady Seraphina, Lady Seraphina, Lady Seraphina.'

~ Say, 'Flame to flame, I call your name. I ask you to come and heal our shame. To heal those wounds for which women were blamed. In my ancestral line I now reclaim. I take back words that did defame. The apple lie, the fall from grace and how beloved Eve condemned us to a hellish fate. I restore the feminine glory, Magdalene's rise, take your place. As this candle burns bright and true, all women of the world, keep your truth shining through.'

~ Send your spirit or consciousness into your Earth Star chakra.

~ Visualize it lighting up so it becomes platinum in colour.

~ A doorway opens in the centre of this chakra gate.

~ Walk through it.

~ Imagine travelling through the soil below.

~ Visualize your consciousness travelling along a tunnel, like the roots of a tree.

~ As you approach the end of the tunnel, you see daylight shining through.

~ It caresses your skin with warmth as you arrive in a beautiful place in nature.

~ You can see smoke rising from what seems to be a campfire in the distance.

~ Lady Seraphina accompanies you as you make your way towards it.

~ The fire is encircled with shells and smooth rocks.

~ Either side of the fire stand two large tipis.

Now, follow these steps for the next part of this exercise, first for your maternal line, and then repeating it for your paternal line:

1. As you enter the tipi on the left, the sweet smell of sage hits you. You find a ring of men and women sitting together around a circle of smouldering rocks.

2. As they turn to smile at you, you realize that you recognize them. Even if you've never physically met, you know in your heart that these are ancestors from your mother's lineage.

3. There's a place in the circle left just for you. You take your place in your ancestral circle.

4. Quietly, each person nods and smiles to acknowledge your presence.

5. One family member is designated as the spokesperson for the healing.

6. Share your findings – your inherited be-LIE-fs with this person.

7. The family peacefully agree that it's time to clear and heal these outdated views.

8. Lady Seraphina gives each person a smooth stone.

9. Each of you sends the energy that you wish to release into the stone, infusing it with your intention.

10. Now, throw your stones onto the pile of rocks in the centre of the tipi.

11. Lady Seraphina hands you a large vat of water.

12. Offer your false be-LIE-fs into this large vat of water.

13. She motions you to pour the water over both the rocks and your stone.

14. The water transforms into steam, symbolizing that a deep transmutation has taken place.

15. Now, you all hold hands and ask Lady Seraphina to heal the Divine feminine wound across all timelines and dimensions.

16. Lady Seraphina clears your ancestors' limited beliefs by sending her flame deep into your Root chakra.

17. See it travelling down into the Earth, and then on to every timeline and dimension.

18. All patriarchy and inherited be-LIE-fs are now cleared from your ancestral line.

19. You say your goodbyes and thank them.

20. Stepping out of the tipi, you feel the warm air touching your face.

You can now enter the second tipi to your right and repeat steps 1 to 20, only this time meeting your father's ancestors. Or, if you need time to process this experience, continue with the steps below and come back to heal the paternal line another time. Do whatever feels right for you.

~   Accompanied by Lady Seraphina, you make your way back to the huge tree from which you descended.

~   Crawl on your belly like a snake, higher and higher up the tree root.

~ You see your Earth Star chakra glowing ahead.

~ Use this gateway to re-enter your body.

~ Take your time settling yourself back into your body.

~ Wiggle your toes to help you to return to the here and now.

~ Take a deep breath.

~ Place your ancestors' gifts that you chose on your altar or on a window ledge.

~ Give thanks to Lady Seraphina and all of your relatives.

Meeting your ancestors on the astral plane can be a very emotional experience. Honour your feelings if you're upset afterwards. Treat yourself with tender loving care, knowing that your loving family are always watching through the veils.

You can bring balance and healing to all of your energy centres by using sound. By having an intention behind a sound, you increase its strength by giving it a direction to follow.

Sometimes it's very obvious that there's an imbalance in a specific chakra centre. Physical and emotional symptoms are the telltale signs. But remember that all energy centres are connected and support each other. Therefore, to top them up, Lady Seraphina advises that you work on all of your centres. You can learn the classic chakra toning chants, or you can create your own healing sound like Lady Seraphina showed me.

Once, I was very worried about having my tooth taken out, so much so that I delayed the appointment for weeks before finally going through with it. During a soul retrieval (a ritual to recover lost fragments of my soul), I discovered that my fear was in fact totally rational. It had triggered a memory of slowly having my lower teeth pulled out in a torture device in a past life. Now I had the reasoning as to why I was terrified, but the fear was still very real.

I knew that my Root chakra was losing a lot of energy over this matter! But Lady Seraphina showed me how to restore it using my voice. She got me to think of a statement that described the situation as already healed. I chose: 'I'm in safe hands.' She then got me to focus my awareness on my Root chakra and say the statement out loud – as if I really believed it and already had it. Next, I went through each chakra making the same statement. I then sealed in the energy by chanting 'Om' seven times.

DIVINE WORD CHAKRA HEALING

This simple step-by-step process will allow you to heal using your voice. Use this formula whenever an issue arises:

~ Call in Lady Seraphina by placing your hands into prayer posture and by calling her name three times.

~ Say, 'Lady Seraphina, Lady Seraphina, Lady Seraphina.'

~ Determine the major chakra affected by the issue – you can discover this by asking your body during a meditation or by choosing the chakra that's physically closest to the symptoms in the body.

~ Spontaneously choose a word or statement that supports the healing of this centre – your body will speak to you.

~ Sitting with your spine straight, focus your awareness on this chakra and state the affirmation out loud to Lady Seraphina.

~ Continue repeating it, introducing more and more conviction within your words.

~ Finally, when you feel ready, make the statement three times to each of the remaining chakras by focusing on them as you say it.

~ Ask Lady Seraphina to seal your words by chanting 'Om' seven times.

~ If the issue resurfaces, talk to the chakra directly and reassure it.

You are what you speak.

The power of your voice teamed with a strong feeling of intention can be used to heal every aspect of your life. Once you've mastered this technique, you'll no longer require any ritual to manifest your desires. The power of word is the mother of all of your Divine powers. Learn to use it and use it with love.

Conclusion

I really hope you've enjoyed this book and, above all, taken away practices to help you to create the most lovely, wisest version of yourself. Now that you know what each Archeiai represents and how they can help you, I urge you to keep up the good work of perfecting your intuitive skills, cultivating a gentle heart and spreading the Divine Word. Remember to tell your friends and clients about the female Archangels. Continue to invite them into your life, your healing practices and your daily affairs. This book is only the beginning. We each hold our own wisdom, which the Archeiai will continue to birth through us. Because of you, their legacy is revived and reintegrated into the planet. The wisdom of the Divine feminine lives on though us.

We are astrologically positioned on the cusp of the Aquarian age (a 2,160-year cycle), which makes this the perfect time to get to know and work with the Archeiai. This is the prophesied time of the feminine rising back into her power. By healing your life and restoring your own sacred feminine essence, you'll receive a head start in smoothly adjusting towards the new paradigm of the great shift. The angels offer us their full support as we step into the acclimatization period of our rapidly changing world.

With our feminine angelic guidance, we're being cleared of what no longer serves, rewired for greatness and prepared for a future of love, balance, health, abundance and integrity.

Through all our mini-victories, our epiphanies, our awakenings and by voicing what was once silenced, we restore Her piece by piece by resurrecting ourselves. That's how amazing and important you are and why the Acheiai have crossed your path; it's also your time.

Enjoy your journey with the female Archangels. Call them in often and they'll see you well.

I wish you all the love, luck and blessings in the world.

Claire x

Glossary of Terms

activation codes – structures of energy that can be used to activate dormant spiritual gifts or higher states of awareness

affirmation – positive statement that can help you to reprogramme your thought pattern, changing the way you think and feel about things

akasha – energy field that contains the akashic records

akashic records – a compendium of all events, thoughts and words that have occurred, stored in the etheric plane

alchemy – a magical process of transformation

androgynous – of indeterminate sex

ankh – a sacred symbol that resembles a cross, having a loop rather than the top arm; popular in ancient Egypt

archeia/i – archangels (chief) consisting of feminine energy

archangels – chief angels

Ascended Masters – human beings who've achieved spiritual enlightenment

ascension – to rise into spiritual power

astral plane – non-physical realm of consciousness

astral travel – travel the non-physical planes of existence in your energy body

athame – ceremonial knife or sword

attunement – the fine-tuning of your energy bodies and chakras to enable them to become a channelling vessel

aura – energy field that surrounds a person, place or object

breathwork – breathing techniques or practices used to promote relaxation, health and deepened states of awareness

Brotherhood of Light – a group of ascended beings who protect the Divine masculine flame

caduceus – a winged staff that has two snakes entwined around it

chakra – wheels of energy around the body that serve as gateways and distribute energy throughout the body

Christos Sophia Gnosis/marriage of the soul – Christos (anointed) Sophia (wisdom) consciousness (receive spiritual enlightenment); Christ is the Heart chakra, Sophia the Crown chakra, and together they help us to achieve the Divine marriage of the soul (balanced in masculine and feminine)

clairaudience – clear hearing; the psychic ability to hear what's inaudible

claircognizance – clear knowing; a psychic awareness of knowledge that you couldn't possibly know

clairempathy – clear emotion; the ability to tune in to places or other people's feelings

clairgustance – clear tasting; the paranormal ability to taste a substance without putting anything in one's mouth

clairsalience – clear smelling; the ability of psychic smell

clairsentience – clear feeling; receiving psychic information through sensing or feeling

clairtangency – clear touching; the ability to retrieve psychic information from touching objects

clairvoyance – clear vision; to gain information through extrasensory perception

comfort zone – a range of conditions in which one feels easy and comfortable

consecrate – to bless and declare as holy

conscious mind – thoughts, memories and feelings that we're aware of at any moment

dimensions (e.g. fifth, fourth, etc.) – Realms of reality, ranges of spiritual consciousness

Divine – of God/dess

Divine Mother – Mother Goddess

Divine Word – the word of God/dess; the word of creation

dreamtime – in a state of dreaming, either when sleeping or when visualizing when awake

ego – the part of the mind that identifies you as separate from Source

enlightenment – the highest spiritual state of understanding

esoteric – spiritual, new age, occult

ESPs extrasensory perceptions – your sixth sense, sensed by the mind

Gaia – Mother Earth

gatekeeper guide – head spirit guide

Grand Central Sun – Helios star gate

guardian angel – an angel who watches over you personally

guru – person who can help you to achieve spiritual enlightenment; dispeller of darkness

Hathor – Ascended Master, incarnated as Hathor, an ancient Egyptian Goddess

Hathors (The) – collective consciousness of the highest initiates of the Divine feminine flame

high vibrational – pure in energy and wisdom

hoodoo – witchcraft

icaros – sacred shamanic songs

indigos – indigo children are those born with spiritual gifts around the 1960s to 1980s

initiation – starting point from which to initiate or begin

instinct – innate feeling

intuition – to understand instinctively

karma – a spiritual law that states whatever you send out returns to you

ki – Japanese for energy; the circulating life force

Kumaras – the sages of Venus

kundalini – life force energy stored at the base of the spine

ley lines – energetic lines that cross the globe and carry supernatural energy

life force – energy of your soul that keeps you alive; your ki

light code – an energetic signature that can awaken and activate your energy

light ray – a being of light who belongs to a spiritual ray (dimension)

lightwork/er – a special person with almost psychic ability to intuit what other people are thinking, feeling or needing in order to heal

lucid dreaming – the ability to be conscious within a dream

moontime – menstruation

Mother/Father wounding – traumatic experiences involving those who raised you that unconsciously affect your relationships with those you encounter throughout your life

negative ion – extra-charged atoms that are good for health; abundant in nature

occult wisdom – hidden spiritual knowledge

overlight – to receive guidance from higher dimensions

paradigm – belief; way of thinking

past-life incarnation - in reincarnation, who you identified as in a previous life

pineal gland – a pea-sized gland in the centre of the brain

power animal – a spirit animal that bestows you with its powers and qualities

power points – places on the land that are high in spiritual energy, such as Glastonbury Tor

quantum physics – science of physics concerned with quantum theory

regression – taken back to recall past-life memories using hypnosis

reiki – Japanese hands-on energy healing

samsara – Sanskrit word meaning being bound to the cycles of life, death and rebirth

sceptre – staff for magic or ceremonial occasions

shadow work – the negative or hidden aspects of the psyche

shaman – a wise man or woman who can access altered states of awareness, such as healing and divination

shamanic – practices associated with a shaman

shapeshift – change physical form, from one to another

Sisterhood of the Rose – an order of the Divine feminine

sixth sense – intuitive faculty

soul – immortal spiritual part of a human or any living thing

soul origin – where your soul first incarnated as a separate entity from Source

soul retrieval – a ritual to recover lost fragments of your soul

Source – God, Creator

superconscious mind – the infinite mind

Tarot – 78 cards used for divination

transmutation – changing from one state of being to another; clearing negative energy

unconscious mind – where the thoughts and feelings that you're not currently aware of reside but can easily be brought into consciousness (for example, memories)

underworld – a spiritual realm where the spirit of power animals, ancestors and nature spirits reside

Unicorn Tapestries – seven woven tapestries from the late Middle Ages that depict the story of the hunt of the unicorn

Venus rose – the path of the planet Venus

void of course – said of the moon, meaning it doesn't have any more major influence or aspect over other planets before it leaves a star sign

witch wound – psychic scar of wounding from the witch trials that still affects the trust between men and (mainly) women across the planet

Yin and Yang – opposite forces of energy; Yin is feminine energy; Yang is masculine energy

Yoni Mudra – hand position that distributes a circuit of energy connecting your consciousness to the womb

yogi – a person who's proficient in yoga

Recommended Reading

Casteneda, Carlos, *The Teachings of Don Juan: A Yaqui way of Knowledge* (NY: Washington Square Press, 1985)

Dispenza, Dr Joe, *Breaking the Habit of Being Yourself* (Carlsbad: Hay House, 2013)

Kenyon, Tom and Sion, Judi, *The Magdalen Manuscript: The Alchemies of Horus & the Sex Magic of Isis*, Tom Kenyon Orb, 2016)

Lister, Lisa, *Witch* (London: Hay House, 2017)

Melchizedek, Drunvalo, *The Ancient Secret of the Flower of Life* (Flagstaff, AZ: Light Technology Publishing, 1999)

Ruiz, Don Miguel, *The Four Agreements: Practical Guide to Personal Freedom* (San Rafael, CA: Amber-Allen Publishing, 1997)

Sadhguru, *Flowers on the Path* (Coimbatore, India: ISHA Foundation, 2007)

Starbird, Margaret, *The Goddess in the Gospels* (Rochester, VT: Bear & Company, 1998)

Starbird, Margaret, *The Woman with the Alabaster Jar: Mary Magdalen and the Holy Grail* (Rochester, VT: Bear & Company, 1993)

Tzu, Lao (trans. Mitchell, S.), *Tao Te Ching: The Book of the Way* (New York: Harper Perennial, 1991)

Ueshiba, Morihei, *The Art of Peace* (Boulder, Colorado: Shambhala, 2007)

Villoldo, Alberto, *Soul Journeying: Shamanic Tools for Finding Your Destiny and Recovering Your Spirit* (Carlsbad: Hay House, 2017)

Warner, Felicity, *Sacred Oils* (London: Hay House, 2019)

Acknowledgements

I feel so lucky and blessed to have been so incredibly supported with this project – more so than you will ever know. With a very full heart, I would like to thank:

John Stone – my hubby, my best mate and my biggest fan all rolled into one. Thank you for your constant encouragement and support. You held every faith in me and served as a firm reminder to believe in myself. Always one to see the grandest vision, you spurred me on to risk everything in pursuit of my dreams. If all failed, you had my back. How amazing are you!

Well, my dream is now realized – I'm an author! Thank you from the bottom of my heart for believing in me, for pushing the boat out, for being flexible and for providing the practical support to allow this project to birth. We are indeed Team Stone!

Leah Jade Stone and **Lexi Faith Stone** – my gorgeous girls, my world. Thank you for bringing out the best in me. You've taught me so much about what life is really about. I know how blessed I am to have a pair of little angels – devils at times but yes, mostly angels. Thank you for being you and for coming to all of my events with the 'hippies'. Thank you for choosing me. This is true love right here.

Monica Cafferky – the best writing coach one could wish for. Thank you for all of your expertise and wisdom in shaping my writing skills. I could never have written that corking book proposal without you! Thank you for helping me to seal the deal with your fabulous strategies. I'm eternally grateful. Our paths crossing was definitely divinely guided. You were part of the angels' plan!

Edward Devlin – my inspiration. Thank you for all of the late-night chats and the incredible practices. I feel truly blessed and honoured to know such an amazing person. I love you and everything that you stand for with all of my heart. God has truly blessed me.

Elaine O'Neil – my incredible editor… what a woman! Thank you so much for everything you do. You're an absolute angel.

Hay House – a massive thank you to all of the staff at Hay House. To everyone who's played a part in the creation of this book, Goddess bless you.

Claire Dean – many thanks for all your expertise and wisdom.

Shout out to my Earth angels – **Sarah Twist**, **Victoria Twist** and **Josie Parr** – for always being there. Love you, girls!

Finally, a big thank you to the people who read this book, to my social media followers, to members of Archangel Alchemy, and to all those who attend Angel Mystery School classes and workshops. Bless you all! May you fly high with the angels.

Keep in Touch

To keep in touch with me, you can sign up to my free monthly newsletter, *Moon Juice*.

An email will land in your inbox a few days before each full moon, allowing you time to gather any bits and pieces should you wish to partake in the rituals and meditations that I provide for the upcoming full moon.

Subscribers also receive an angel oracle message, a spiritual blog, astrology reports, rituals, events, offers and so much more!

Sign up at www.clairestone.co.uk

Over on my blogs section you'll discover a wealth of topics that you can use as part of your spiritual toolkit.

You can also follow me here:

 Claire Stone, Ancient Wisdom Modern Woman

 Claire_Stone_444

 Claire Stone

Events

All of my events are posted on both my Facebook page and on the Events section on my website.

Angel Mystery School®. For all your angel training, you can find more at: www.clairestone.co.uk

Online Subscription

To delve even deeper into the realms of the angels, I offer a 13-month online course membership called Archangel Alchemy®. Each month, we'll work with a specific Archeia and Archangel.

You'll receive a guided meditation, a downloadable angel information pack and a 60-minute live online session. To find out more, fly over to www.clairestone.co.uk

Online Courses

Angel Communication Online Course

Teaching

In person, I teach the following:

- Angel Communication Course

- Psychic Protection Masterclass

- The Female Archangels

- Healing with the Archangels

- Sisterhood of the Rose

- Manifesting with Mojo Bags

- Manifesting with Sigil Magic

- Drum Journeying with Mugwort

ABOUT THE AUTHOR

Miriam Rajčániová

Claire Stone is a writer, international psychic reader and spiritual teacher. Born with the ability to see and hear spirits and angels, she began giving readings at the age of 14 and went on to host her first event at The Chalice Well in Glastonbury, England, when she was just 19.

Claire qualified as a holistic therapist and has professional qualifications in herbalism, aromatherapy, reflexology, reiki, crystal therapy, and ancient Egyptian magic and ritual. She's an initiated Priestess of Mary Magdalene, Sisterhood of the Rose. Claire now hosts workshops and retreats that are designed to equip participants with tools and techniques to reawaken their gifts and to empower themselves, creating a happy and fulfilled life led by the soul. She is the founder of Angel Mystery School® and offers various accredited training programmes.

Claire lives in St Helens, Merseyside, with her husband, two daughters and two dogs, Minnie and Milo.

f Claire Stone,
Ancient Wisdom Modern Woman

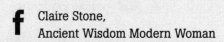 Claire_Stone_444

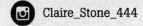 Claire Stone

www.clairestone.co.uk

HAY HOUSE

Look within

Join the conversation about latest products,
events, exclusive offers and more.

f Hay House

🐦 @HayHouseUK

📷 @hayhouseuk

🖤 healyourlife.com

We'd love to hear from you!